FOCUS ON SPORTS

FOCUS ON SPORTS

Photographing Action

by

RICHARD TURNER

AMPHOTO
American Photographic Book Publishing Co., Inc.
Garden City, New York

Second Printing, March 1976

Cover graphics based on the following photographs: *Frank Gifford* photo © 1960 Ziff-Davis Publishing Company. Reprinted by permission. *Motocross racer* photo by Steve Reyes. Reprinted by permission. Other photos by author. Frontispiece photo of Sandy Koufax, former ace Los Angeles Dodgers pitcher, by Ernie Schworck, UPI.

Library of Congress Catalog Number—74-79256
ISBN—0-8174-0577-1
Manufactured in the United States of America.

CONTENTS

For Beverly, Janet, Nancy, and Michael

ACKNOWLEDGEMENTS

Many generous people have aided in the preparation of this book. It would have been impossible to complete without the invaluable help given me in a number of different sports by my fellow photographers whose credits appear under their pictures. I am also indebted to the following persons for their unselfish willingness to share with me, over the years, their immense knowledge in the field of sports photography: Phil Bath, Elmar Baxter, Bill Beebe, Bill Brunk, George Brich, Herb Carleton, Don Cormier, Bob Flora, Hal Filan, Steve Hansen, Harley Martin, Harry Matosian, Ben Olender, Felix Paegel, Charles Poalillo, Art Rogers, Carlos Schiebeck, Larry Sharkey, Mike Smith, Roger Squire, Vic Stein, and Ernie Schworck.

A special word of thanks to Jack Sheedy and George Long, West Coast photographers for *Sports Illustrated,* whose time and effort have been freely and graciously given in the checking and rechecking of information and data and whose encouragement throughout the labor of writing the manuscript has been deeply appreciated.

Special editorial assistance was provided by photojournalists Don and Dana Downie and Lou Jacobs. Veteran outdoorsmen Gus Newman, Mike Kizziah, and Dave Severson of Laurence Laurie and Associates, Los Angeles, California, offered excellent suggestions on coping with the intricacies of horse shows and rodeos, as well as fishing with both rod and camera. Steven Lescher, Public Relations Counsel for Los Angeles Memorial Coliseum and Sports Arena, made it possible to successfully complete many difficult assignments.

Additional pencil-sharpening aid came from Paul Ulmer Photo Lab, Los Angeles, California, and Leo North, Panorama City, California, in preparing the section on black-and-white films and developers. Earl Tanner of Gibbons Color Lab and Mel Felix of GP Color, Los Angeles, California, contributed their gems of guidance on working with color.

Finally, a tip of the lens cap to Hal Jensen, retired dean of *Los Angeles Examiner* sports photographers, whose kindness and guidance to the author as a teen-ager covering his first high school football game helped make this book possible.

To all of you, a most sincere thanks.

Richard P. Turner

INTRODUCTION

Behold the sports photographer. . . . He is wet, cold and miserable kneeling on the sidelines of the football stadium at Hometown Tech. Icy showers of rain have shorted out the motor drive of his Super-Zilchflex, in spite of its protective plastic wrapping. He is reduced to thumbing one shot at a time, as in the Speed Graphic days of another generation dimly remembered.

No athlete is he. Football is a tedious game he can tolerate only when viewed on television in the warm comfort of his neighborhood pub. The sight of a bunch of overgrown adolescents battering each other on a rain-washed gridiron leaves him as cold as the late autumn air he is freezing in. He is a sports photographer only by virtue of his editor, who has handed him credentials stapled to the assignment slip and ordered him out into the dismal afternoon. But he is a professional, and the rain dribbling down his neck is ignored as he squints through the viewfinder, doggedly waiting for *the* picture that tells the story of the game. One moment . . . one play . . . maybe a speedy running back knifing his way through a swarm of would-be tacklers or maybe a pair of rangy ends leaping high in the air for a pass. It will come as a sudden burst of action, there before him in $^1/_{1000}$ sec., then gone forever. Unlike his sportswriting brethren, the photographer gets no second chance. There are no erasers in cameras.

If you are interested in taking a shot at sports photography for fun or as part of your professional work, you will find it exciting. It differs from other forms of photography in one important way — the photographer has little or no control of the events before him. He does his best to anticipate action that will provide dramatic photos. But this is only guesstimating the situation. He must remain constantly on the alert, finger poised on shutter release, gauging the exact instant to get the picture.

There are many opportunities and many markets for sports photography. Pick up almost any publication, and you will usually find some type of coverage of a sports event or personality. Why? In our leisure-oriented society, people have more time to devote to sports and recreation, whether as participants or simply as spectators. Witness the fantastic growth of professional football, baseball, basketball, hockey, and auto racing in recent years. Sports news is eagerly read in a multitude of newspapers and magazines. There is also a whole new world of monthly publications catering to the special interests of boat, golf, ski, auto, motorcycle, and tennis enthusiasts, to mention but a few.

You don't have to be a professional press photographer covering major league sports events to get spectacular photos. Your local high school, small college, neighborhood little league, YMCA, or even merchant and industrial teams will provide all the action you can handle. By applying professional techniques that will be discussed in the following chapters, you will score with many good shots.

A program of sports photography will sharpen your vision and have you operating your camera with the utmost skill. You will find that the mechanical processes of advancing the film, focusing, and shooting will become reflex actions, leaving your mind free to concentrate on the sport.

If it turns out that you don't really dig sports and prefer more sedentary photographic activities, you will have gotten a lot of exercise and fresh air. So you win either way.

CHAPTER 1

SPORTS PHOTOGRAPHY FOR THE AMATEUR

Successful sports-action pictures depend on a combination of skilled camera technique, good judgment, and luck. If you know a particular sport well, it is possible to anticipate the moment of action that will provide dynamic pictures. If it's an event with which you're not thoroughly familiar, try attending a few games as a spectator to gain understanding of some of the action commonly seen, like the line plunges, passes, and end runs in a football game. This will give some idea of what to expect when you take your camera to the playing field.

Reading advance stories in your local newspaper or asking a friend who is knowledgeable about a sport can also help. Chances are you will only need to do this a few times before learning the fundamentals.

Adequate preparation is essential to good sports pictures. Before you go out to shoot an event, take a moment to think about the kind of action that will take place and what you want to show. It is a good idea to arrive at the playing field or stadium well in advance of the starting time. Scout the area to determine the best possible camera angles. Figure out where you are going to locate and the type of equipment necessary to do the job. Careful planning will help you gauge the right moment to shoot when the action begins.

Sports events are usually unpredictable, and you won't always be able to plan your pictures. There are certain basic situations in every sport, however, that can be turned to your advantage. For example, in baseball, with a runner on first base who is taking a long leadoff, it's a pretty safe bet that he will try to steal second base if he can. Should the runner stray too far from the bag, the pitcher may attempt to pick him off with a quick throw to the first baseman. You will have a picture situation with either the runner diving to the ground while attempting to elude the tag or electing to dash for second and possibly being caught in a force play between the two basemen. This is an example of how knowledge of a sport's fundamentals can help you be ready when the action gets hot.

Where can an amateur photographer go to shoot pictures like this? Coverage of major college and professional events is nearly always restricted to accredited press photographers, but amateurs are usually welcomed at local little league, high school, small college, or semipro games as long as they don't interfere with the players or officials. If you are interested in covering a specific event, it is a good idea to contact school or league authorities in advance. They will frequently go out of their way to help you. It doesn't hurt to send them a few prints of your best shots in exchange for courtesies received. This is always good public relations.

If it's an event that's being broadcast on your local radio station, having a pocket-size transistor radio with an ear plug will keep you tuned to the action at all times. This is especially helpful in identifying players with whom you are unfamiliar. Sports announcers are a pretty savvy bunch and can help you understand what is happening out on the field.

Sandlot or playground games have a great potential for special human-interest shots. These informal games are not as strictly regulated as the school or professional events. Here you can get close to your subjects without too many restrictions.

In summary, here are a few basic rules to remember:

1. Learn something about the fundamentals of the sport you will be covering.

2. Be thoroughly familiar with the mechanical functions of your equipment so you can concentrate on the sport.

3. Plan your shooting location and your equipment in advance as much as possible.

4. Make sure that you don't get in the way of the players and officials or that you don't block the vision of spectators. Keep off the playing field at all times.

5. Expect the unexpected. The outfielder may drop a pop fly, the quarterback may fumble the ball, the racing cars may collide, and so on. By staying alert, you will have a better chance to capture on film the split-second action that tells the story.

CHAPTER 2

TOOLS OF THE SPORTS PHOTOGRAPHER

CAMERAS AND LENSES

Good sports pictures can be made with almost any type of camera. There is a tremendous array of equipment on the market available to the photographer. The most important consideration is interchangeable-lens capability. This allows use of normal, wide-angle, or telephoto optics to meet the requirements of the sport. Fixed-lens cameras usually limit the photographer to fairly close-up situations. In some sports like basketball and track, this is not a problem as long as it is possible to work along the sidelines. If this cannot be done, then a fixed-lens camera is a serious handicap. Other sports like football, baseball, and auto racing fairly demand the use of long lenses. The photographer with a fixed, normal focal-length lens seldom gets a crack at the really exciting action.

Cameras suitable for sports use are of three main types, excluding press and view models. The 35mm single-lens reflex (SLR) with through-the-lens viewing is favored by most professionals. It lets you see exactly what you get on film, and the present generation of SLR's features a wide range of interchangeable lenses and other goodies: instant-return mirrors; built-in, automated exposure systems; and motor drives for rapid sequence shooting. The SLR is also available in the 2¼″ (120/220) film format for those who prefer to work with a larger negative.

SLR automatic lenses are a valuable aid. The image is focused with the lens wide open. When the shutter is tripped, the automatic diaphragm takes over and stops the lens down to the correct aperture an instant before the film is exposed.

The rangefinder camera is fast to use, easy to focus in dim light, and usually smaller and lighter than the SLR. The viewing and rangefinder functions are combined in a system that is mechanically linked to the lens, and this may lead to problems. Many potentially great photographs have been taken with the lens cap accidentally left in place or a finger in front of the lens. In this case, the optical viewfinder shows a lovely, bright image that unfortunately never gets on film.

Normal, wide-angle, and medium-telephoto lenses, up to 135mm, are well suited for use with 35mm rangefinder models. Longer focal lengths will not couple to the rangefinder because of its built-in optical/mechanical limitations. They require a supplementary reflex housing, which, in effect, converts the rangefinder camera into a single-lens reflex. These attachments are usually clumsy to use and may cost more than a standard 35mm camera body.

Rangefinder cameras of the 2¼″ variety are also available. Because of their larger rangefinder optics, they can handle longer lenses than the 35mm models, up to focal lengths of 250mm on some models.

The 2¼″ twin-lens reflex has enjoyed a great deal of popularity for more than 40 years. This camera has two identical fixed lenses — one for viewing, the other for taking the picture. Some cameras offer interchangeable lenses with shutters built in between the lens elements. The chief drawback with this type of camera, as with the 2¼″ rangefinder models, is that it is impossible to fit extremely long telephoto lenses (300mm and up) without expensive modifications by a skilled photographic technician.

One more type of camera deserves recognition — the press models such as the American Speed Graphic, the German Linhof, and the Japanese Horseman. They are hand cameras utilizing a bellows attached to a heavy-duty frame and offering interchangeable lenses of

(Above right) Remote-control motorized Nikon was mounted in front of cockpit of Glastron/Molinari outboard racing boat driven by Dick Sherrer. Note the cord running from camera into cockpit with trigger device attached to steering wheel. Sherrer was able to photograph himself during a practice run on Lake Havasu, Arizona, before start of the Outboard World Championship. This system was used to back up radio-control unit that triggered camera from shore. (Right) Hulcher 70mm sequence camera operates at 5 or 10 fps at shutter speeds up to 1/2000 sec.; frame rate can be increased as high as 50 fps on some models. The camera is custom-built, it uses heavy-duty batteries, and it can be adjusted to use lenses of major photographic manufacturers. The Hulcher 70mm sequence camera requires bulk loads (100 feet) of 70mm film, and is used mainly by large news organizations (AP and UPI) and major magazines for important sports events.

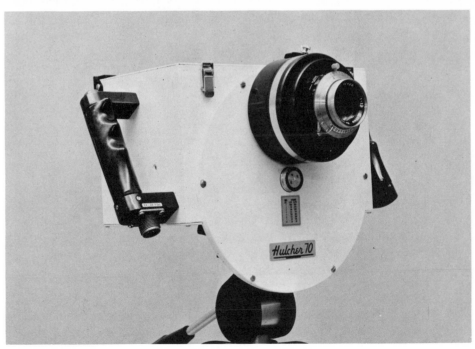

varying focal lengths. Focusing is accomplished with a rangefinder coupled to the lens, or on some models, through a groundglass at the rear of the camera with the shutter open on "Time." This second method is very precise but also *slow*, as the shutter must be closed and reset to the desired speed after the lens is focused. It is more suited to the studio than the sports arena.

Press cameras are made in film formats from $2^{1}/_{4}''$ to $4'' \times 5''$ and can handle both roll and sheet films. Sheer weight and bulk make them unsuitable for fast operation, but they fill a need for situations where a large-format negative or transparency is required. The $4'' \times 5''$ Speed Graphic was the badge of the working newsman for many years until major technical improvements in 35mm cameras, lenses, and films made it obsolete. They were great cameras in their day, and in the hands of skilled photographers, produced some of the finest news and sports pictures of our century.

The fledgling sports photographer soon learns that some equip-

Hulcher 35mm sequence camera offers great rapid-fire capability to the sports photographer. It may be adjusted to operate as fast as 20 fps at shutter speeds up to 1/4000 sec. The camera is custom-built, is operated by heavy-duty batteries, and it uses bulk loads (100 feet) of 35mm film.

The sports photographer of earlier generations had to carry a lot of heavy equipment to do his job well. Hal Jensen, *Los Angeles Examiner* staff photographer and sports specialist, unloads 4″ × 5″ Speed Graphic cameras from the trunk of his car in this 1946 photo. He is reaching for an early model Wabash/Sylvania strobe light, whose bulky power pack is visible in box at right. Behind it is a 4″ × 5″ Graflex with a 15-inch 375mm telephoto lens. Compare this hardware with modern, lightweight 35mm cameras currently in use. Photo by Don Downie.

ment is better suited for certain jobs than other equipment.

The widely used 35mm single-lens reflex is usually equipped with a focal-plane shutter, offering top speeds of $^1/_{500}$ sec. or $^1/_{1000}$ sec. Some models go as high as $^1/_{2000}$ sec., offering great action-stopping capability. Most focal-plane shutters are very accurate and dependable. Their principal weakness is inability to synchronize with strobe lights at speeds greater than $^1/_{60}$ sec. or $^1/_{125}$ sec. because of construction and design limitations. This can be a problem when strobe is used in strong available light. (Example: color shots at a boxing match where the ring lighting is directly overhead and flash is needed to fill in the shadows.) The strobe flash will halt the action of the fighters, but the slow shutter speeds might produce a blurred, secondary, or ghost, image on the film, with the main strobe-image sharply etched upon it. Such results are seldom acceptable to editors.

Although cameras with focal-plane shutters are preferred for general sports coverage, they are not perfect for all situations that may arise. In the case of the brightly lighted scene, a camera equipped with a between-the-lens or leaf shutter, synchronizing with strobe up to its fastest shutter speed, is recommended for best results. Most professionals maintain a wide variety of equipment in their photographic arsenals to cope with problems.

The choice of lenses depends on the sport you will be covering. In some sports a 200mm or 300mm telephoto is essential, while in others a normal to wide-angle lens is all you'll ever need. Since lenses often represent the major share of the photographer's capital investment, they should be selected with great care. Buy the best quality lenses you can afford, but don't automatically rush to acquire the newest, fastest lens on the market. If most of your sports photography occurs during daylight hours at outdoor events, a super-speed lens is not necessary. Fast films can be used to make up the difference in low-light situations. The faster the lens, the more it costs to manufacture, and the higher price is passed along to the customer. It pays to think ahead as to how you're going to use your equipment. By purchasing a slightly slower lens, you can use the money you save toward the purchase of additional lenses to build your outfit.

Whatever lenses you buy, take test shots at all apertures to determine which aperture produces the sharpest negatives. Be sure to include tests with the lens wide open. You may have to shoot this way at some future event if the light is poor. Most reputable photo dealers will let you buy equipment on a ten-day, money-back trial basis. This is ample time to shoot tests and learn how well a camera and lens perform.

When buying lenses, beware of very cheap bargains. They often prove unsatisfactory for really critical work. There are exceptions to every rule, but in photography, as in most businesses, you usually get what you pay for.

In selecting additional lenses for your camera, it is a good idea to start with a telephoto about double the focal length of the normal lens. Most 35mm cameras are sold with a 50mm or 55mm lens for general use. A 100–135mm lens is very handy for most sports. Later on, the serious photographer will want to buy a 200–300mm lens to provide a still longer reach. Beyond these lengths are the extra-long (and expensive) 400–600mm optics, which are useful for special situations where it is impossible to get by with shorter lenses. (Example: covering a baseball outfielder in action if you're shooting from the grandstand.) For the 2¼″ man, the normal 75mm or 80mm lens may be augmented by telephotos of 150mm, 180mm, 250–300mm, and up.

Telephoto lenses, besides putting you right in the middle of the action, can be useful, creative tools. They pull things together in a way that the human eye never sees by exaggerating perspective and compressing space. This has the effect of making near and distant objects seem much closer together than they really are. If used properly, telephoto lenses can produce very dramatic pictures.

For the photographer who prefers the convenience of a single, long lens that adequately covers the most important focal lengths, a telephoto zoom is recommended. They are available in a wide variety of combinations. The 80–200mm or 80–250mm zoom is probably the most versatile. There are shorter (50–135mm) and longer (200–600mm) combinations offered by various lens manufacturers to cover almost any situation.

Unfortunately, telephoto lenses, zooms included, have drawbacks that create photographic booby traps. Focusing the image is critical, especially at wide apertures. Depth of field is much shallower than with a normal lens. The longer the lens, the less the depth of field at any given aperture. The really long telephotos (400mm and up) are usually quite heavy and difficult to hand hold. Camera movement is likely to degrade image sharpness. A sturdy tripod is helpful, but it can also be a hindrance by anchoring the photographer to a fixed location. For fast-moving sports, like football, a monopod is much better, especially when following action from the sidelines. It provides most of the tripod's steadiness and far greater mobility.

Zoom lenses have their own special aberrations, including barrel distortion (straight, vertical lines rendered as curves) and focus shift while zooming from short to long focal lengths. These faults are minimized in the better-quality lenses, but they can be an irritating problem in some of the less expensive models on the market.

If you're considering a zoom lens, buy it on a conditional basis if possible, allowing adequate time to shoot a few rolls of film at all focal lengths and apertures. Any major defects will quickly become apparent. More than most lenses, zooms seem to follow the "apples in a barrel" theory — some are better than others.

Wide-angle lenses are an important part of the sports photographer's equipment. They offer a fine way to achieve power and drama in your shooting and widen your horizons by showing the broad sweep of an event. The photographer can relate subjects to their surroundings more effectively with a wide-angle lens than he can by backing off a subject with a normal lens.

The wider the angle of the lens, the greater its depth-of-field characteristics. Focusing is far less critical because of the increased zone of sharpness between background and foreground. This may prove troublesome when focusing some single-lens reflex cameras in bright light. The lens shows so much depth that it is difficult to tell where the point of critical focus really is. However, the broad zone of sharpness will usually take care of minor focusing errors.

Along with these virtues, some wide-angle lenses are prone to distortion of the image at the edges of the picture. If you are not careful about composition, wide-angle lenses will also show too much dead space in the foreground, requiring severe cropping in printing.

The ultra-wide optics (20–28mm in the 35mm format) can produce really wild distortion in subjects close to the camera. This distortion is not always desirable when photographing people, but it can lend impact and drama to an ordinary scene. For example, an extreme wide-angle lens can make a racing sailboat look longer and more exciting than it really is.

There is a great variety of excellent wide-angle glassware available to the 35mm photographer including fisheye lenses, offering almost full-circle coverage. The 20mm, 24mm, 28mm, and 35mm focal lengths are very effective in sports work. For a $2^1/_4''$ camera, you might consider lenses in the 40–65mm bracket for comparable results.

VIEWFINDERS

The camera viewfinder best suited for sports work is one that accurately shows the field of view of the lens. Most reflex and rangefinder cameras presently on the market have excellent viewfinder systems, but there are others around whose viewing optics leave much to be desired when photographing fast-moving subjects.

Some of the early rangefinder cameras manufactured before and immediately after World War II had smaller tubular viewfinders. These viewfinders reduced the image size to such an extent that it was very difficult to follow action and gauge distance. Recognizing the limitations of their viewing systems, the manufacturers offered accessory optical finders that produced an enlarged field of view.

George Long, *Sports Illustrated* photographer, uses a monopod to steady his motorized Nikon with 400mm telephoto lens at a pro football game. He is also equipped with another Nikon with 200mm lens to cover action at closer distances. Monopods are favored by sports photographers; they offer the mobility needed for a fast-moving assignment where a tripod is not practical.

These viewfinders were further refined by the addition of parallax-correcting optics that could be set to keep the subject centered at different distances. If, for example, the lens was focused on a subject at 30 feet, the viewfinder was manually adjusted to that distance—simple and effective but time-consuming.

Modern rangefinder cameras take care of this chore instantly with bright-frame, parallax-correcting viewfinders. Of course, the SLR's with through-the-lens viewing eliminate any parallax worries. Some SLR's feature interchangeable viewfinders and offer the photographer a wide choice of focusing screens to suit individual tastes. Equipment-wise, we've come a long way in a few short decades.

MOTORIZED CAMERAS

The motorized-sequence camera has become standard equipment for the sports-oriented pro. Capable of firing several times per second, the motorized camera gives him some fine opportunities. By shooting a sequence on a fast-moving situation, the photographer has a better chance to get exactly what he needs. Editors can pull one story-telling shot from a sequence or run several pictures to illustrate an event.

Good sports pictures can be made without using a motorized camera. When the action heats up, however, the photographer gets only one chance, not several, for a spectacular picture that an editor will use. And that, after all, is the name of the game. With standard equipment, too often the photographer will shoot a split second too soon or too late. Even if he times his shot perfectly, at the peak of action, something more exciting may happen an instant later; and he can't get it. The motorized camera reduces this possibility. By filming a burst of action from start to finish, little is left to chance.

Some purists may sneer at the motorized technique as making sports photography too simple. But the fact is, editors don't care how the pictures were made as long as they are available when required. For the professional, earning a living with a camera is tough work, and any tool that makes the job easier is worth using. Besides, using a motorized camera does not automatically assure good results. It is still possible to miss the best picture by being out of phase with the action. How is this possible?

Most sequence cameras utilize a battery-operated electric motor drive operating at 2–4 frames per second. Let's suppose you are shooting a high jumper in a track meet. If you simply start snapping away as he commences his run, chances are good that you will miss the exact instant he clears the bar! The exposures may take place a fraction before or after he is at the apex of his jump—even at a shutter speed of

^{1}/$_{1000}$ sec. While this is an extreme case, it has happened.

The best way to use a motorized camera is to aim for the peak of action as if you were using standard equipment but to keep on shooting until the action is dissipated. This method will usually produce excellent results. It will also conserve film. If you hold the shutter release down on a sequence camera operating at 3 frames per second, you will expend a normal 36-exposure load in 12 seconds, and you may be left holding an empty camera when something dramatic happens.

Besides rapid-fire sequences, a motorized camera can be used effectively for single shots. You never have to move the camera away from your eye to manually advance each frame. In an action situation, each shot can be made selectively, if desired, by pressing the release at the decisive moment.

A number of top manufacturers offer 35mm SLR sequence cameras. Motorized versions of the Canon, Leicaflex, Minolta, Nikon, Olympus, Pentax, and Topcon are widely used. And with the growing demand, several other manufacturers have future plans in the works for making sequence equipment. For the 2¼″ photographer, the Hasselblad is available with an optional electric motor drive.

The custom-built Hulcher sequence camera is the sports photographer's heavy artillery. Designed around a unique, rotary shutter, the Hulcher uses 70mm or 35mm film and is powered by heavy-duty batteries. The sequence speed can be adjusted from 5–20 frames per second. Because of its costliness, the Hulcher is used mainly by photographers on assignment from major magazines and news organizations — *Sports Illustrated*, United Press International, Associated Press, and others. The Hulcher-equipped photographer can cover the fastest action imaginable with complete confidence. He is sure to come up with at least one frame that shows the peak of action.

The Hulcher can be adapted to use lenses of major photographic manufacturers. Its only drawback, besides expense, is that it uses bulk loads (100-foot rolls) of 70mm or 35mm film, requiring special processing equipment.

REMOTE-CONTROL DEVICES

Most motorized cameras can be adapted for remote-control operation by devices ranging from a simple, extra-long cable release to a complex, radio transmitter-receiver combination capable of tripping the shutter at distances of a mile or more. This capability opens a whole new world for the imaginative photographer. Remote-control cameras have been mounted on airplanes, race cars, motorcycles, boats, and even on missile launching pads to record the beginning of a space flight.

In an action situation where it is physically impossible or dangerous for the photographer to obtain closeups, remote-control devices may be used to let a cooperative subject take his own picture! The popular Nikon SLR, for example, has a simple plug-in receptacle in its motordrive unit. A connecting cord with release button—even an ordinary household door buzzer—can be run from the motor to a predetermined position. It can be as long as is necessary.

The fisheye color photo of outboard racer Dick Sherrer was made during a practice run at Lake Havasu, Arizona, in preparation for the Outboard World Championship, which is held there each year.

These swift, single-seat racing hulls are constructed with satin-smooth fiberglass or mahogany. There are no handholds of any sort, and it would have been suicidal to attempt to ride the craft during an 80 mile-per-hour speed run on Lake Havasu.

A motorized Nikon was mounted in front of the cockpit on a jerry-built rig, secured by rubber suction cups and heavy-duty marine tape. A 10-foot cable release was fabricated from household wire with a standard plug on one end and a door buzzer on the other. It was taped to the hull of the boat, extending into the cockpit, with the buzzer/release secured to the steering wheel. It was a simple matter for driver Sherrer to photograph himself during the practice run with his companions.

A radio transmitter-receiver unit, triggered from shore, was also used during the photo session, but continuous pounding from the speeding racer caused it to malfunction after a few rolls. The simplified door buzzer/release was then reinstated to complete the job.

From this take came a full-page color shot in a newspaper Sunday magazine, another full page in the outboard race program, and many black-and-whites used in newspapers and boating publications throughout the country.

Remote-control operation can be a photographer's ace-in-the-hole when the assignment can't be accomplished by conventional methods.

BLACK-AND-WHITE FILMS AND DEVELOPERS

There are a great many black-and-white films available, and most professionals tend to standardize on one or two that will handle almost any assignment. A fast, general-purpose pan film like Kodak Tri-X is a wise choice. It has ample speed (ASA 400) and latitude to cope with the wide range of lighting conditions encountered in sports work. When properly exposed and developed, it will produce negatives with surprisingly fine-grain structure and excellent tonal range. Its high speed makes it especially useful for photographing sports action under low light levels. With special processing, it may be pushed to speeds of ASA

The Minolta SR-M, a 35mm single-lens reflex motor-drive camera.

1000–1600 without objectionable loss of quality. Tri-X is also less contrasty than the slower emulsions such as Plus-X or Panatomic-X. It can safely handle harsh lighting situations like strong sunlight on snow in a winter sports scene. (For the recommended processing technique see page 143). Ilford HP4 film, a British import, has many of the characteristics of Tri-X and is also popular with some photographers.

Whatever film you choose, it is best to determine your ASA ratings by personal tests because of variations in camera shutters, exposure, and development procedures. A soft-working, fine-grain developer like D-76, Microdol-X, Ethol UFG, Promicrol, or Microphen will produce good-quality negatives. There are many other developers not listed that will yield equally good results.

For pushing films shot under available-light conditions, Acufine developer is often the choice of press and magazine photographers because of its ability to deliver high speed ratings (ASA 1200–1600) without excessive grain. Many press photographers also favor Kodak HC-110 developer for both pushing and general use because of its processing speed.

Kodak D-23 is an old-time, commercial photographer's formula that is not sold in prepared packages but must be hand-mixed from bulk chemicals. It is a soft-working developer with great compensating action—the ability to produce excellent shadow detail without blocking the highlights. Kodak's D-23 gives outstanding gradation and moderately fine grain. It is especially useful with slower films, like Plus-X, for negatives exposed under very contrasty lighting. Here is the formula:

KODAK DEVELOPER D-23

Water, about 125° F.	24 ounces
Kodak Elon Developing Agent	$1/4$ ounce
Kodak Sodium Sulfite, dessicated	3 ounces, 145 grains
Cold water to make	32 ounces

Dissolve chemicals in the order given. To start, develop the Plus-X for 6 min. at 68° F., and the Tri-X for 9 min. at 68° F. These developing times are for guidance only and may be adjusted to suit individual preferences for negative densities.

There are far too many developers for the average photographer to test personally. Most professionals not only standardize on one or two films, they settle down with one or two developers that will fit their needs. A photographer might choose a good, general-purpose "soup" (slang for developer) like D-76 for normal use and a high-energy developer like Acufine for pushing. This is a wise procedure for the amateur to follow. Use the developer recommended by the film manufacturer, then try a few others and compare the results.

Experiment if you must, but for simplicity, find a developer you like and stay with it. Once you learn its characteristics with your favorite film, it is easy to produce negatives that will yield top-quality prints.

COLOR FILMS

Choosing a color film is largely a matter of personal taste. One film may be great for a particular assignment and unsatisfactory for another. Some sports photographers swear by Kodachrome 25 for its color contrast, sharpness, and super-fine grain. Others swear at it because its super-slow speed (ASA 25) limits its use to fairly good lighting. Because of its complex emulsion structure, Kodachrome 25 can only be processed by Kodak or a commercial lab licensed by the manufacturer. It is

The fast-handling 35mm single-lens reflex camera is favored by most professional photographers who cover sports assignments. A wide variety of single-lens reflex equipment, including telephoto-zoom lenses, is shown in use by photographers covering the California 500 auto race at Ontario Motor Speedway near Los Angeles. One photographer aims his camera through a hole cut in the fence by track officials to accommodate photographers at certain preferred locations on the turns.

definitely not for the photographer who likes to control every facet of his color developing. But if you can live with its slow speed, Kodachrome 25 will deliver outstanding quality. When processed by the manufacturer, it is the most consistent of all color films from one lot to the next.

Need more speed? Try Kodachrome 25's sister film, Kodachrome 64. At ASA 64 you gain a full stop, but overall color rendition is not quite as faithful as the slower emulsion. Even so, Kodachrome 64 is an excellent all-purpose film. Ektachrome-X, also ASA 64, gives beautiful, saturated colors, but it is not quite as sharp as the Kodachrome emulsions. However, its speed can be doubled in processing without excessive color shift or increase in graininess. Ektachrome-X has good latitude and may be processed by Kodak, a custom color lab, or the photographer if he purchases the required chemicals. Kodak also provides a special processing service to boost the speed of Ektachrome-X.

When the light is low, High Speed Ektachrome (Daylight), ASA 160, is very useful. It can be exposed at ASA 320 or ASA 400 with adjusted processing. Pushing to these higher ratings may result in some loss of definition and increased graininess. There may also be a pronounced color shift with blacks turning greenish as well as unpredictable effects with other colors. Nevertheless, the High Speed Ektachrome (Daylight) will let you shoot sports action under terrible lighting conditions. It is also available in Type B emulsion (ASA 125) for indoor work under tungsten light. The speed can be boosted to ASA 320 if necessary.

Color negative films such as Ektacolor Professional Type S (ASA 100) and Kodacolor II (ASA 80) are used when color prints are needed quickly. They will also produce acceptable black-and-white prints, but the quality is not quite up to the standard of prints made from black-and-white films. Many newspapers use color negative material for ROP (run of press) color reproduction on major sports events.

Besides Kodak, fine color films are available from photographic manufacturers throughout the world. Agfachrome (Germany), Ferraniacolor (Italy), Fujichrome (Japan), GAF (U.S.A.), and Ilfocolor (England), all have their enthusiastic users. You may try these films and compare them with your favorite brand. As with black-and-white films, it's a good idea to standardize on one or two color films to achieve consistent results.

FILTERS

Many professionals keep a UV (ultraviolet) filter on each lens to protect it from dirt and scratches. This filter can be used for any color or black-and-white film without requiring exposure increases. It is, in effect, a lens cap through which you can shoot.

The UV filter absorbs excessive ultraviolet light in sea, snow, and mountain scenes. It cuts through distant haze, reducing the bluish cast of color transparencies shot on a cloudy day. The 1A Skylight filter is very similar. It has even greater ultraviolet screening action and produces warmer colors.

Some skylight filters require a minimal (one-half stop) increase in exposure with color film. They work well with black-and-white too, usually without the need for any adjustment of exposure. Follow the manufacturer's instructions for the filter you are using.

Color conversion filters permit outdoor use of indoor color film (with an 85A) or indoor use of daylight color film (with an 80B). They are extremely valuable when you can't finish a roll in one lighting situation before moving to another.

Most black-and-white sports work is done without correction filters (except for the UV or Skylight). Occasionally, an outdoor scenic is required, and the photographer's best friend is the old standby medium-yellow (K2) filter to darken the sky and emphasize clouds. It corrects most panchromatic films so the subject appears as the eye sees it. An orange (G) filter produces considerably more contrast and renders the sky darker than the K2. A light-green (X1) filter is excellent for outdoor portraits because it emphasizes skin tones and lightens green foliage.

The red (25A) filter makes skies extremely dark and is good for dramatizing backlighted or silhouetted subjects. These basic filters call for exposure increases of one (K2), two (X1, G), and four stops (25A). Exposure adjustments may vary slightly with filters produced by different manufacturers.

For special purposes there are polarizing, diffusion, and neutral-density filters. The polarizing disc lets you darken a blue sky without affecting the other colors in an outdoor scene. Diffusion filters cut the sharpness of a lens to secure a veiled, dreamy effect if you wish to be arty, and neutral-density filters decrease the speed of black-and-white or color films. They can be lifesavers in very bright situations, such as beach or snow scenes, when the film is too fast for the job and you can't stop down your lens far enough to prevent overexposure.

CHAPTER 3

ACTION SHOOTING SIMPLIFIED

FOCUSING

Focusing a lens on a rapidly moving subject is a difficult chore that requires considerable practice. In some sports, like auto or motorcycle racing, it is nearly impossible. For this reason, experienced sports photographers rely on a zone-focusing system, which assures them of a very high percentage of sharp negatives. Here is the way it works.

Simply prefocus the lens where you expect the action to take place —such as the line of scrimmage in a football game or the finish line in a track meet—and let the depth of field of your lens work for you. It is necessary, first of all, to know how your lenses perform at various apertures and focusing distances, as well as the area or zone where you will have everything sharp on your film. For example, let's consider a 135mm f/3.5 telephoto lens on a 35mm camera, a typical combination used by many sports photographers. With the lens set at f/11 and focused on a subject 50 feet away, the depth of field, according to the manufacturer's instruction sheet, will be a comfortable 38–72 feet. At f/5.6 it is reduced to a belt that ranges from 43–59 feet, still good; but wide open at f/3.5, the depth of field is reduced to 48–55 feet. This means a slender, seven-foot area of sharpness from the farthest subject to the nearest subject. Translated into practical terms, focusing at the maximum aperture is critical. If the manufacturer's instruction sheet is not available, you can work out your own depth-of-field information for any lens by shooting a test roll.

Normal and wide-angle lenses usually give far more depth of field at any given aperture and focusing distance than the telephoto variety. If you can get close enough to the action, there is no problem. However, if you are shooting from a distance, the shorter focal lengths give you such tiny images that the photos will be worthless, showing excessive grain and lack of definition when enlarged.

For easy handling of telephoto lenses with the zone-focusing system, try this method. First, put some white, plastic, or adhesive tape around the lens barrel next to the focusing mount, making sure you don't impede its function. Suppose you are covering a baseball game; take a position midway between home plate and first base (or between home and third), keeping clear of the base paths the runners will use. Focus on first base, and mark the tape with a line or arrow opposite the footage scale. Repeat this for home, second, and third. Your tape can be marked with a "1" for first base, "2" for second, and so on. Don't forget to include the pitcher's mound and the team dugouts, in case some interesting action develops at these locations. You will not be able to cover the outfield unless you have extremely long lenses. An exception to this would be a junior league game for youngsters where the field is smaller and distances are proportionately reduced.

Use as many marks as you need, prefocusing each one. Remember that this technique depends on the camera remaining at a fixed location. If you move around, the marks will not be accurate. You will have to refocus visually. If a runner breaks from first to second, you can quickly move the focusing mount from "1" to "2", and your lens will be in sharp focus to catch him sliding into the base. If the action shifts to third, a short twist of the lens to position "3" and you're in business.

In the beginning, it may seem difficult to move the lens to the designated marks, raise the camera, and shoot. With a little bit of practice, you will find it very easy. As time goes on, you probably won't even have to take the camera from your eye, gauging the required movement of the lens mount by feel as you watch the image snap into focus. For normal use, the tape-on-lens-mount system works admirably. It can be adapted to almost any sports event where you are working from a fixed camera position. But some sports photographers refine this technique even further by having a camera technician construct a compact gear shift arrangement to move the lens forward and backward with tiny movable stops that can be preset to various distances.

SHUTTER SPEEDS

Selection of the proper shutter speed is determined by the requirements of the sport. If the subject movement is broadside, or crossing directly in front of the camera, a top shutter speed of $1/500$ sec. or $1/1000$ sec. is necessary to stop the action. An example is a football game in which the ball carrier and defending players run parallel to the camera position. If you move down the sidelines about 10 yards ahead of the line of scrimmage, the action will be coming head-on, or at about a 45-degree angle. A moderately fast shutter speed of $^1/_{250}$ sec. would be adequate because the players are traveling a shorter distance across the film. If you were to shoot fast broadside action at this speed, the image would be blurred. As a general rule, always shoot as fast as your film and the available light will permit. But remember, it isn't always necessary to shoot at $^1/_{1000}$ sec. By using slower shutter speeds whenever possible, you will be able to use smaller apertures and create a greater depth of field, a precious commodity in action shooting.

PANNING

You can make a $^1/_{100}$ sec. or $^1/_{125}$ sec. shutter speed perform like $^1/_{1000}$ sec., stopping fast, broadside action as well as creating graphic visual effects!

How? By the old newsman's trick of panning the camera with the action. Panning is accomplished by moving the camera smoothly and steadily to keep the subject centered in your viewfinder. As the subject passes in front, press the shutter release but follow through by keeping the camera moving as the subject speeds away. If properly executed, the subject will stand out sharply against a blurred background, suggesting the excitement of great speed.

In the early days of press photography, when films were slow and cameras were not equipped with fast shutters, panning was a necessity. Photographers had to master this technique to survive. Nowadays, you have the option of utilizing panning to avoid the monotony of completely frozen action in every picture. If you're really steady, you can use shutter speeds as low as $^1/_{30}$ sec. or $^1/_{15}$ sec. to further blur the action, thus heightening the feeling of speed. However, these slower speeds are tricky to use until you are thoroughly experienced in panning; there is too much chance for uneven camera movement that will ruin the picture. A good starting point for pan shots is $^1/_{100}$ sec. or $^1/_{125}$ sec. Either speed will stop a surprising amount of action and blur the background adequately. As you gain more experience with this technique, you can experiment with slower speeds to achieve some really wild blur. The visual effect is beautiful, especially in color.

Practice panning without film in the camera. Find a busy street and follow moving cars, keeping them framed in your viewfinder. As the cars pass directly in front, gently squeeze the shutter release and follow through by keeping the camera in motion. You will find it necessary to prefocus the lens at the point you wish to shoot.

A tendency for the inexperienced photographer is to shoot too soon, before the subject is centered properly. A few practice sessions will eliminate this error. Try to locate a camera angle where the action will be moving in a horizontal sweep across the film plane. The subject does not have to be at a complete right angle to the camera, but it should be as close to a right angle as possible to permit some broadside panning motion. Try to keep the subject centered in the viewfinder.

Panning, when properly executed, will let you shoot fast-moving subjects, such as runners in a track meet or boat, automobile, and motorcycle races, with excellent results. Try it, but don't overdo it. A succession of endlessly blurred action pictures, no matter how arresting at first, soon becomes boring. Keep this valuable technique in mind when you need a change of pace to complement your conventional stopped-action coverage.

This flat-track motorcycle race was covered from a balcony seat in the grandstand. In this head-on shot of four motorcycles, the shutter speed was lowered to $1/8$ sec. and the camera was panned to create a feeling of great speed. Data: Nikon, 135mm lens, Tri-X rated at ASA 1600, available light, developed in Acufine.

CHAPTER 4

LIGHTING

AVAILABLE LIGHT

Outdoor sporting events present few lighting difficulties. There are numerous fast films and lenses available to handle any conditions that may arise. However, many of the most popular sports events are held outdoors at night under floodlights (baseball, football, track, automobile, motorcycle racing) or indoors at arenas (basketball, hockey, boxing), and photographing these presents problems.

A dependable exposure meter is a necessity in addition to a basic knowledge of film processing at increased ASA ratings. Consider a possible situation in a dimly lighted sports arena. Your camera is loaded with fast pan film, normally rated at ASA 400. A meter reading indicates an exposure of $1/60$ sec. at $f/2$. By rating the film at ASA 1200, you extend the exposure range by two full stops. This permits shooting for $1/250$ sec. at $f/2$, a more practical shutter speed for fast action. The film must be processed in a high-energy, soft-working developer, like Acufine or Ethol UFG, to work effectively at the higher ASA rating. There is a limit to pushing film. Severe overdevelopment is likely to cause excessive grain and contrast, making it difficult to obtain top-quality prints. Follow the manufacturer's recommendations for the film and developer you use.

Shooting sports by available light offers many advantages. Unhampered by lights and sync cords and not worried about flash guide numbers, you are free to move around and find interesting angles. If you are fortunate enough to be working in a well-lighted gymnasium or arena, available light may be the best way to operate. It is frequently the most flattering light to the subject, bringing out the physical form and adding depth to the picture in a manner that cannot easily be duplicated with artificial lighting.

STROBE

When the available light is too low for even the fastest film, experienced sports photographers turn to electronic flash "strobe" to get the job done. There are a great many small portable units on the market, most of which are excellent. The heavy-duty strobes (Ascor, Honeywell, Metz, Norman, and so forth), using rechargeable nicad or replaceable dry-cell batteries, are recommended because of their increased light output and their fast recycling times. The weight of the power pack and flash head varies from 1–12 pounds, depending on the size and power (50–200 watt-seconds) of the strobe.

The tiny, cigarette-pack size strobes, so popular with many photographers, are usually 40 watt-seconds, or less, and featherweight. However, their low light output limits you to a shooting range of 12–15 feet. The larger strobes are considerably heavier and more expensive, but they let you work at greater distances or stop down the lens for increased depth of field.

Some photographers like to use two or more strobes for spectacular, multiple-light photos at indoor events, synchronizing them with connecting wires or small slave trippers (photoelectric cells that will fire all units simultaneously).

Major magazines, like *Sports Illustrated*, will often light a sports arena with a battery of huge A/C strobes so their photographers can shoot color as easily as black-and-white. These elaborate installations are very costly and may take two days for a crew of technicians to set up. The results are usually outstanding, but such complex electronic projects are beyond the scope of the average cameraman. Most sports events may be adequately covered with much simpler equipment when available-light pictures are not practical.

FLASH

The lowly flashbulb has been pushed far into the photographic background by the development of dependable, low-cost strobe lights. Flashbulbs can be used only once and are expensive, costing 10 to 20 cents each. They do offer certain advantages for the sports photographer. Most focal-plane shutters on 35mm cameras will only synchronize with strobe at $1/50$ sec. or $1/60$ sec. This is slow enough to cause blurred ghost images when photographing a moving subject in bright sunlight. A small flashgun, with a folding fan reflector and a pocketful of peanut bulbs, neatly solves the problem of fill-in lighting when you need it to knock out a shadow area. The fan reflector may be folded to reduce the light output for closeups. Moreover, you have the opportunity to use very large flashbulbs in the rare instances where a lot of light is needed. You are not stuck with the fixed light output of a strobe unit.

Most focal-plane shutters will synchronize with flashbulbs up to $1/1000$ sec. Although you can shoot almost anything in pure daylight, these compact flash units can help you overcome occasional shadow problems where some fill-in lighting is required at a fast shutter speed.

Cookie Lavagetto, whose pinch-hit double with two out in the ninth won the fourth game of the 1947 World Series, is lifted on the shoulders of jubilant Dodger players. Data: 4" × 5" Speed Graphic, fast pan film, flashbulb. UPI photo.

CHAPTER 5

ANTICIPATING SPORTS ACTION

Making Your Own Luck

There is definitely an element of luck in sports photography, but the professional, who makes his living with a camera, does not depend on it. He does his best to provide his own luck by knowing his equipment and the fundamentals of the sport to be covered. By understanding a sport and knowing its rules, he can concentrate on getting the picture.

Part of this knowledge comes from taking an interest in the local teams and athletes he may be called on to photograph. Radio and television broadcasts and the sports pages of a newspaper can help tremendously.

One year during football season, I was assigned to get pictures of a high school league-championship game for a local newspaper. Having followed the progress of both teams throughout the regular season, I knew that the reserve quarterback of one school was a very strong passer, who could throw the long bomb in clutch situations. Armed with this knowledge, I was prepared when the coach sent him into the game late in the fourth quarter with the score tied 7–7. Anticipating a long pass, I moved down the field, ahead of the line of scrimmage, and was in position when the young quarterback unleashed a magnificent 50-yard throw that floated into the outstretched arms of his receiver, who raced through a swarm of defensive tacklers into the end zone with the game-winning touchdown.

The picture ran six columns wide in the home edition with my credit line in boldface type underneath it. The sports editor said nice things.

Two weeks later, the same team was playing in the state high school semifinals. Flushed with confidence and intent on covering every play, I watched for the moment when the quarterback would be sent into the game. Sure enough, another tie score brought the youngster off the bench and into the lineup. Again I moved downfield and waited for the big play. The ball was snapped from center; the quarterback tucked it under his arm and faded behind a cluster of blockers. I was so intent on looking for a pass receiver that I completely missed his behind-the-back hand-off to a speedy fullback, who raced around the opposite side of the line of scrimmage and down the far sideline for a touchdown. The home team won, but I lost that picture.

In anticipating action, you'll be wrong a good deal of the time; but by staying alert and concentrating on the game, you will bag a large percentage of good pictures.

Another good way to make your own luck is to try something different. If you are covering an event and have made a number of safe action shots, ones you're fairly sure of, look around for unusual angles, subjects, or something else that will set your picture apart from those made by other photographers who may be present. Don't forget the spectators. Stop every now and then and look around you. There are people everywhere, and they are all part of the drama of sports. Frequently, the antics of the fans tell the story better than the action on the field.

Remember, also, that some of the action in any sport will not photograph well. For instance, a key play may be too far away for the lens you are using, or you may be in the wrong position at that moment. If you are planning to shoot for publication, cover yourself by filming the athletes before the event, perhaps on the bench, in the team dugouts, or in the pit areas at motor-sports contests. A telephoto lens is handy for making candid shots of top players while they rest or warm up. You will at least have these shots if an action shot is impossible.

All too frequently, some athlete will perform a great deed that wins an event and catapults him to instant fame. Unless you were lucky enough to get him during the event, your only chance is to shoot him afterward amid all the tumult and shouting. These scenes of triumph can be pure hell for photographers caught in the crush of a wildly cheering crowd that swarms onto the playing field. You just have to get in there and do the best you can. Many fine victory shots have been made by the "Hail Mary" method—holding the camera overhead, tilting it down slightly, squeezing the shutter, and praying that you have captured the triumphal scene somewhere near the center of the negative. A motorized camera with a wide-angle lens is a great help in this type of situation.

CHAPTER 6

BASKETBALL

Basketball is one of the most popular sports in the United States. You will find it played at nearly every high school and college as well as at professional games in the larger cities. Coverage of major college and professional games is usually restricted to working-press photographers. However, amateur lensmen are nearly always welcome at local high school and small college games.

In addition to schools, your neighborhood church, YMCA, or recreation center may have teams engaged in local competition. There are also merchant or industrial leagues that offer additional picture-taking opportunities. In some parts of the country, basketball is practically a year-round sport.

In order to get good shots, you need an alert eye, a quick trigger finger, plus an understanding of the sport. The action in a game is lightning-fast. Knowing the fundamentals will help you to anticipate the split second of action that can mean a great picture.

You don't need expensive equipment. Almost any focusing-type camera with a shutter speed of at least $1/200$ sec. or $1/250$ sec. and a normal focal-length lens will do the job. If you aim to do much available-light work, you'll need at least an $f/3.5$ lens. However, these features are usually standard even with modestly priced cameras.

Fast panchromatic film, like Tri-X, will make it possible to obtain excellent, available-light action shots even under extremely low light levels. A dependable, small strobe unit, however, is a valuable accessory because the available light may not always be adequate in some situations. This is especially true at some of the smaller high school and college gyms.

To cover a game with your normal lens, take a position at the corner of the court in line with the basket, from 15–25 feet away. The camera should be prefocused on a point under the basket, since most of the action will take place in this area. You can get many good shots as the team with the ball tries to score, and you also capture the tricky, defensive floor play by the opposing team as they maneuver to block scoring attempts.

Another excellent location is a spot directly behind the basket, about 15 feet in back of the court boundary line. The action will usually be coming head-on. Normal or wide-angle lenses that are used from this position and show the players and part of the crowd in the background can produce dramatic results. Be careful though! Fast-charging players occasionally run out-of-bounds and may land in your lap if you don't move out of the way.

Telephoto lenses will permit a greater choice of pictures. You can achieve some interesting effects by working from a higher angle in the grandstand. An 85–135mm lens on a 35mm camera will produce good shots from a considerable distance. This is especially important if you want to shoot at major college or professional games. Only accredited press photographers are allowed on the sidelines of the court. These events are usually staged in well-illuminated arenas where available-light shots present no problem. Try to get a first-row balcony or aisle seat, if possible. If you shoot from the middle of a crowd, excited fans may jump in front of your lens during a crucial play.

A good method of operation is to cover the first half of a game from an overhead position, then go down on the court and work from the sidelines, or as close as you can get to the action. This will insure against having a bunch of monotonous pictures all from the same angle.

Fast exposures are essential in basketball photography. A minimum shutter speed of at least $1/250$ sec. is advisable. However, it may not always be possible to shoot that fast due to low light levels or slow shutter speeds of your camera. It is still possible to make good shots simply by timing the exposure for that peak of action when motion is arrested. An example of this is the tip-off at the start of the game, when the centers of both teams jump for possession of the ball that was thrown in the air by the referee. You can make this shot easily at $1/100$ sec. or $1/125$ sec., if you are careful to hit the exact instant when the players are suspended in mid-air at the top of their leaps. The best camera angle for the tip-off is from the side of the court, opposite the center position.

During the course of the game you'll have ample opportunity for peak-of-action pictures. Catch the players leaping into the air to shoot a

(Pp 40-43) When available light is clearly inadequate, a strobe light is needed to ensure printable negatives. In this series, a 100 watt-second strobe was bounced off a light-colored gymnasium wall behind the photographer at a high school basketball game. It was possible to obtain evenly illuminated action shots as the players jumped, ran, and wrestled for possession of the ball. This method avoided the harsh, flat lighting a single flash at the camera would have given. However, it is only possible when there is a suitable wall close behind the photographer, with no spectators or other obstructions in the area. Data: Rolleiflex, 80mm lens, 1/250 sec. at f/5, Tri-X. Exposure was adjusted for bounce-strobe technique, requiring a 2 1/2-stop increase as compared to direct strobe on camera.

basket or grabbing the ball as it rebounds off the backboard. Even some of the lightning-fast plays have moments of suspended action, permitting slower shutter speeds.

A player dribbling the ball down the court toward the opponent's basket encounters defending guards who block his forward progress. He pivots and stops, searching for a teammate in the clear to whom he can pass the ball. The tense facial expressions of the athletes, poised for instant movement, will make a very effective picture.

Available-light action shots require careful exposure and development for best results. It is a good idea to arrive at the game early and shoot a test roll. This can be done while the players are taking their warm-up shots during the pregame practice session. Use your meter, and make a series of exposures according to the existing light. The test roll should be processed first to guide you in handling the actual game pictures. You will probably find it necessary to rate your high-speed film at exposure indexes of ASA 650–1000 to operate effectively under existing-light conditions.

If the existing light is clearly inadequate, you are much better off using a strobe light than fighting "available darkness." There are many small, inexpensive strobes on the market that are ideal for basketball photography. Proper exposure will vary according to the power and light intensity of the model used. Follow the manufacturer's instructions for the best results.

Multiple-strobe lighting adds to the dramatic quality of your pictures. Athletes look better if illuminated from the sides or rear. The additional lighting creates a feeling of depth and modeling that is far superior to the single-flash-at-the-camera shot. If your strobe has provision for a secondary extension light, take advantage of this by placing the unit on the side of the gym facing a basket, about 10–20 feet from the camera at a 45-degree angle. The light and wire should be taped down or otherwise secured so that nobody will trip over it. If there are spectators seated behind the basket, you may not be allowed to place additional lights in this area. Officials usually will not object as long as there is no hazard to players or spectators.

Slave lights, triggered by photoelectric cells, are great, providing there are no other photographers present who are using flash. Every time they take a picture, your slave will fire too, and it may not have recycled at the moment you decide to shoot.

A good method of working with a single light is to bounce it off a wall or reflector placed in line with the basket. However, this technique is dependent on the physical layout of the gym; there has to be a wall or balcony to which the stanchions supporting the basket are attached. Also, there must be no spectators seated in this area.

All-American basketball center Bill Walton, U.C.L.A., stuffs the ball into basket to score against USC. The photographer climbed to a catwalk high above the court at Los Angeles Sports Arena to make this unusual action shot. Data: motorized Nikon, 300mm lens, 1/250 sec. at f/4.5, Tri-X rated at ASA 1000, available light. Photo by Richard Mackson, Santa Monica Evening Outlook.

I have had good luck working in this manner with a light-color gym wall acting as a natural reflector. If the wall was dark, I simply taped a 2′ × 3′ section of white matteboard to the wall for increased lighting efficiency. If you try this system, make sure your strobe is powerful enough to handle long-range bounce shots by making tests. Some of the midget units currently in use just don't put out enough light for this somewhat unorthodox, but effective, technique. Bounce lighting, or even bare-bulb strobe (if your flash reflector is removable) will help eliminate the flat, uninteresting lighting typical of single-flash pictures. You will retain the quality of available light while throwing in just enough fill to open the shadow areas. Again, for the best results, shoot a test roll following the manufacturer's exposure instructions.

Don't get so engrossed in shooting the action that you forget to take an occasional glance at the spectators. Tensions run high during a game, and excited fans display a variety of emotions ranging from ecstasy to black despair. Candid pictures, showing the frenzied antics of the crowd or the coach and reserve players sweating it out on the sidelines, will round out your coverage of the sport.

A sports photographer has many opportunities for interesting feature shots, like these high school cheerleaders performing at a basketball game. Data: Minolta, 35mm lens, 1/125 sec. at f/4, Tri-X rated at ASA 1000, developed in Acufine.

CHAPTER 7

BASEBALL

Baseball, the great American pastime, is not too difficult a subject to photograph. Outside of professional league games, you can usually work along the sidelines of the playing field as long as you don't interfere with the conduct of the game. This means staying well behind the base paths at all times. Keep one eye on the batter, even if you are concentrating on action elsewhere on the field. A sizzling foul ball may be heading your way when you least expect it.

Potentially, every player is a good subject—the pitcher with his long, deliberate windup; the batter tensed to swing, his bat cocked and ready; the catcher crouched low, waiting for the throw. The ball sails in and the batter swings, his body twisted far to the side. There are three moments when this action rates a picture: (1) when the batter commences his swing; (2) when the bat connects with or misses the ball; and (3) when the batter completes his swing.

You will need a very fast shutter speed to show the bat making contact with the ball, at least $1/500$ sec. To catch this at the exact instant, you must anticipate the action somewhat. Trip the shutter as the batter swings. If you are lucky, you'll stop the ball in mid-air somewhere inside the batter's box. This action occurs in a split second, and is almost too fast for the eye to follow.

A medium-long telephoto lens (135–200mm on a 35mm camera) is handy for sideline work, allowing you to pull in the action from a safe distance. Shooting the outfielders in action will be interesting, but you'll need very long lenses (400–600mm) to obtain decent negatives, unless it's a junior or little league game on a smaller diamond where the shooting distance is greatly reduced.

The immortal Babe Ruth's final appearance on a baseball field at Yankee Stadium, New York. Winner of the 1949 Pulitzer Prize for news pictures, the Graflex Diamond Award, and many other honors, this picture is an all-time great. It has been reproduced in newspapers, magazines, and books throughout the world. Data: 4″ × 5″ Speed Graphic, 135mm lens, 1/25 sec. at f/5.6, Kodak Super Panchro-Press Type B, cloudy, dark afternoon light. Photo by Nat Fein, New York Herald-Tribune, courtesy of Wide World.

A good method of coverage is to stay between home plate and first base until a player gets on base. You have both areas in view if there is action. With a runner on first, move to a position slightly to the right of the bag. If the runner takes too long a leadoff, the pitcher might attempt to pick him off with a quick throw to the first baseman, or he might try to trap the runner into a force play between first and second base. This often produces a wild scene as the runner dives headfirst for the bag in a frantic effort to elude the tag.

High school baseball games can provide a great many action shots, like this runner attempting to reach home plate on a teammate's single. Note the ball in mid-air at runner's side and catcher poised to receive the throw while the umpire watches intently. Shot from a position near first base where it was possible to cover action at either location. Data: Nikon, 200mm lens, 1/1000 sec. at f/4, Tri-X, cloudy afternoon light. Photo by Herb Carleton.

(Above) A classic among baseball pictures, it shows outfielder Al Gionfriddo making the catch that saved the day for the Brooklyn Dodgers, forcing the 1947 World Series into the seventh game with the New York Yankees. Data: 5″ × 7″ "Big Bertha" Graflex, 40-inch 1000mm telephoto lens, Eastman Type B pan film. Photo by Edward Jerry, UPI.

(Right) A runner steals third base and is safe by a wide margin as the third baseman waits in vain for the throw. Shot at a minor league pro game from a location about halfway between home plate and third base, a good spot for covering a play at these two positions. Data: Leica, 135mm lens, 1/500 sec. at f/8, Plus-X, late afternoon sunlight.

51

Action at second or third base is likely with a man on first. These positions are best covered from a point about midway between home plate and third base. You will be able to shoot a runner attempting to steal second base. If the batter hits a long ball and the runner goes to third, you are ready if he slides into base.

To cover second base from the sidelines on a regulation-size field, you'll need at least a 300mm lens, preferably longer, otherwise negative images may be too small to enlarge properly. Press photographers covering baseball normally use telephotos of 400mm and longer for this type of work. Most major league games are covered from special camera positions located in the grandstand, press box, or at ground level near team dugouts. League regulations prohibit photographers from roaming the sidelines while a game is underway.

At day games in bright sunlight, players' faces are often partially hidden by shadows caused by the peaked caps that they wear. There is not too much you can do about this except try for pictures showing form and action rather than facial expressions. Sometimes, a low, ground-level camera angle will minimize distracting shadows enough for the players to be identified. If the game continues into late afternoon when the sun is at a lower angle, you have a better chance of illuminating players' faces.

To show the pitcher in action, shoot from behind home plate, where you can frame him between the catcher and batter. If there is a wire screen barrier, try shooting through an opening in the wire.

If it is too small to poke a lens through, use a moderately wide aperture (f/5.6–f/8) to help dissolve the image of the wire and keep it from appearing in the picture. This technique requires that you keep at least the center portion of your lens unobstructed and is more effective with telephoto lenses than shorter focal lengths because of their greatly reduced depth of field. You may find it necessary to switch to a slower film to avoid stopping down the lens past f/8. Smaller apertures will make the wire too visible.

If there are troublesome reflections from the wire at your camera position, eliminate them by wrapping black masking tape around the wire. This will prevent flare from spoiling the shot.

Night baseball is often difficult to photograph properly because of extremely low light levels, even in some of the major league stadiums. Under these conditions, aim for moments when the action is momentarily arrested, as when a batter is poised to swing or as he follows through. Other possibilities include a pitcher ready to throw or a runner taking a lead off a base. By concentrating on situations where the players are not actually in motion, you can make good pictures that suggest violent action and capture the mood of the sport.

Little League pitcher John Kay, 10, displays big-league form as he unleashes his fast ball in a game at Woodland Hills, California. Shot through wire screen behind home plate to give a batter's-eye view of the action. A moderately wide (*f*/5.6) aperture of a 200mm lens prevented the image of the wire from appearing in picture, because the center portion of the lens was not obstructed. Data: motorized Minolta, 200mm lens, 1/1000 sec. at *f*/5.6, Tri-X, hazy-bright sun in late afternoon.

Headlong slide by runner into second base was not quite fast enough to beat the throw on an attempted steal. Shot was perfectly timed to catch the ball in mid-air, just before it reached the second baseman's glove. Action in a junior college game was covered from sidelines with a 300mm telephoto, the minimum focal length required for shots at this location on a regulation-size playing field. Data: Nikon, 300mm lens, 1/1000 sec. at f/8, Tri-X. Photo by Herb Carleton.

CHAPTER 8

BOXING

In boxing, there is no substitute for a ringside seat. Even then, there are many difficulties with which to contend. You are restricted to the assigned seat and cannot move around during a fight. Ropes and ring posts may interfere with camera angles; you must shoot around and through them as best you can.

At important professional fights, most first-row ringside seats are reserved for working newsmen. Anyone else buying a ticket could be placed as far back as 20 rows. Some fight promoters are notoriously liberal in their definition of "ringside." Without press credentials, your best chance for boxing photos is at the smaller fight clubs staging semi-pro or amateur events. You may be able to wangle a choice seat in return for some action shots that the management can use for publicity purposes.

The normal method of shooting a fight is to aim the camera through the ropes while leaning forward on the narrow ring apron in front of your seat. Since the action is seldom more than 15–18 feet away, the normal lens of your camera will do nicely. Many boxing photographers like to keep a second camera with a wide-angle lens ready for a speedy grab shot if the fighters move in close.

Boxing action is fast and furious. You must be able to focus and shoot quickly, manipulating camera controls by feel. The fighters are constantly in motion, maneuvering for an opening and seeking a weak point in their opponent's defense. They weave, feint, and jab in rapid succession. Then there may be a sudden flurry of action as the fighters trade blows. Aim for the peak of motion as the gloved fists land, and

(Right) The bell sounds, the two fighters advance to the center of the ring, eyeing each other warily, each man intent on striking the first blow. Data: Nikon, 50mm lens, 1/250 sec. at f/2.8, Tri-X rated at ASA 1200, low light level at ringside from overhead floodlamps in semipro fight arena, developed in Ethol UFG.

(Below) Action at its peak is captured in this dramatic shot of current heavyweight champion Muhammed Ali pounding challenger Ken Norton with blows to the head. Note the spray of perspiration flying above Ali's gloved fists. Norton won by a decision in this 1973 bout at Los Angeles, California. Data: Nikon, 180mm lens, 1/250 sec. at f/4, Tri-X rated at ASA 800, strong available light at ringside from overhead floodlamps. Photographer was 50 feet away, shooting from rear of press section. Photo by Richard Mackson, Santa Monica Evening Outlook.

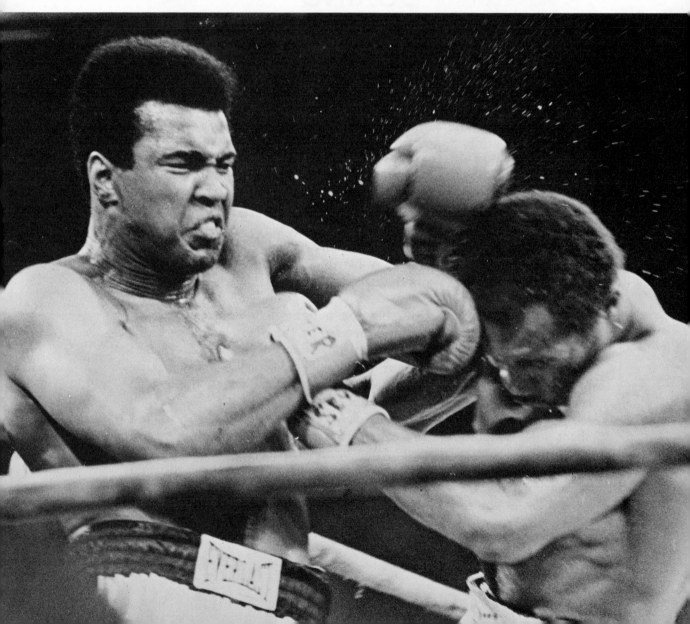

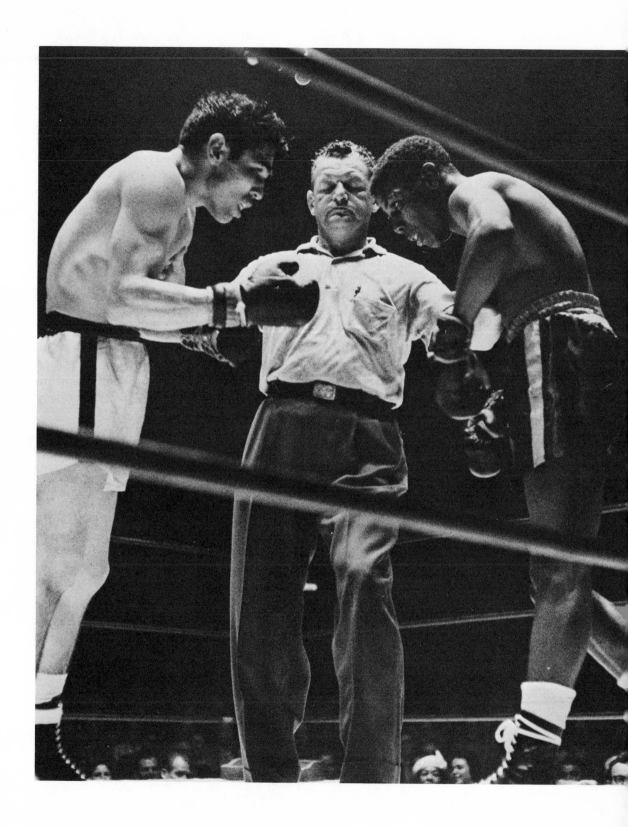

then for a fraction of an instant, are stationary before being withdrawn. You must watch for this nearly invisible instant, anticipate it, and trip the shutter.

Another example of arrested motion in the ring occurs when a fighter ducks under a jab or hook. The two men will be almost still as the punch traveling its full distance stops in mid-air and the ducking fighter halts his downward movement. The contorted facial expressions of the combatants will make a fine shot.

The third man in the ring, the referee, may step in front of the camera at anytime as he moves around the fighters. If this happens, just grit your teeth and try again. There's nothing you can do about it. For this reason, a large newspaper or magazine might assign as many as five photographers to a championship fight—four men stationed around the ring and the fifth in an overhead location in the stands with a long lens. Someone will be sure to have a clear shot at a moment of crucial action.

The dramatic climax of a fight arrives when a man is knocked out. If your camera angle and timing is good (and the referee doesn't block the shot), you will capture the moment of bruising impact as the punch connects and the dazed fighter crumbles to the canvas. The classic instant of boxing unfolds as the referee bends low over the victim, tolling off the count while the other fighter retires to a neutral corner.

As the count reaches 10, the referee steps around the fallen opponent and lifts the winner's gloved hand in the traditional symbol of victory. At this point, the crowd normally erupts in a tumultuous ovation as the fighter's manager and trainers swarm into the ring to congratulate him. Occasionally, a victorious fighter is lifted on the shoulders of his handlers or fans and paraded around the ring—another good opening for an impressive picture.

Knockouts, though spectacular, really don't happen too often. Most boxing matches end in a decision, the winner having been selected by a panel of judges on the basis of points scored for fighting ability.

Natural lighting in the ring is often quite pleasing. In most arenas and stadiums where fights are held, the ring is lighted by powerful flood lamps placed directly overhead. The canvas floor is usually an off-white or gray color that yields great reflectance, filling in shadow areas from below. With fast pan film pushed from ASA 800 to ASA 1200, you may be able to shoot at speeds up to $1/500$ sec. with apertures around $f/2.8$, depending on the illumination of the individual arena.

At the smaller fight clubs or gymnasiums, the ringside lighting is generally too dim from the standpoint of picture quality; a strobe is needed to insure printable negatives.

When you are calculating exposures at ringside with a reflected-

Sugar Ray Robinson knocks out Bobo Olson. Data: 4″ × 5″ Speed Graphic, fast pan film, three strobe lights mounted above the ring. UPI photo.

light or through-the-lens meter, powerful overhead flood lamps may cause exaggerated readings that can get you in trouble. Blindly following the meter may lead to a batch of badly underexposed film. Proper exposure is based on the flesh tones of the boxers. You may have to open up one or two stops over the indicated exposure to get adequate detail in their faces.

Boxing is hard to photograph well, requiring a lot of film and probably more good luck than most other sports. The difficulties are there, to be sure, but they can be overcome by thought and effort.

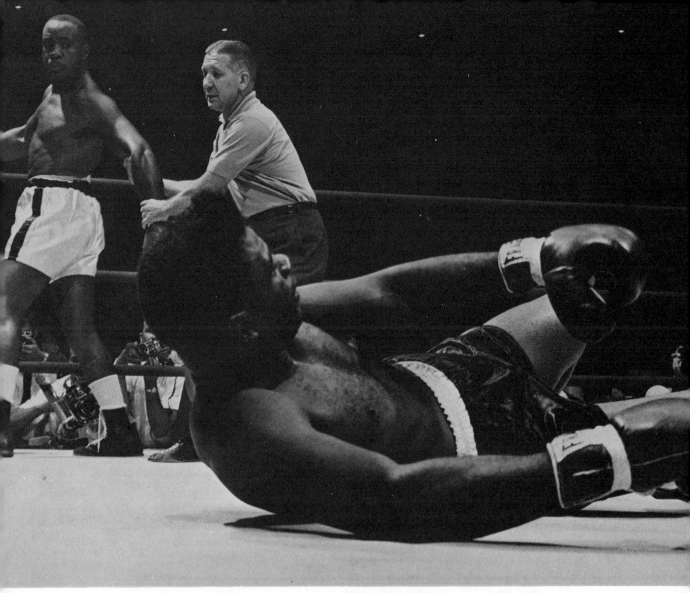

Floyd Patterson lies on the canvas after being knocked out by Sonny Liston in a heavyweight title bout at Las Vegas, Nevada. As the referee moves him toward a neutral corner, Liston looks back at his fallen foe. Data: Nikon, 35mm lens, 1/250 sec. at f/4, Tri-X rated at ASA 800, available light from floodlamps above ring. Photo by Carlos Schiebeck, UPI.

CHAPTER 9

FOOTBALL, SOCCER, AND RUGBY

FOOTBALL

If you are the kind of photographer who enjoys shooting fast, violent action, you'll find many worthwhile subjects at football games in the fall. As in covering most sports, a knowledge of the fundamentals is helpful because you have to second-guess the quarterback and anticipate the direction of every play. You'll be wrong at least half the time, but if you know what is happening out on the field, your chances of capturing a spectacular picture are greatly increased.

Football can be covered from both the ground level and the stands (with long lenses). Photography from the sidelines is hard work, especially in those punting duels where the ball moves from one team to the other at opposite ends of the field. At most games, photographers are permitted to work from the end zone up to the 35-yard line, on either side of the field. But to prevent distracting the coaches, photographers are not allowed in front of the player's bench. At some major college and professional league games, one photographer from each newspaper or wire service may be allowed to work in front of the bench at the discretion of the coaches. This privilege is usually restricted to those newsmen who have early deadlines to meet. Normally, photographers are required to stay behind the bench when moving down the field. Also, learn and obey the standard ground rules for photographers that are in effect at most stadiums throughout the country.

1. Stay in back of the sideline boundary stripe at all times; keep off the playing field. At some stadiums, photographers must also remain behind a second boundary stripe, three to six feet from the sidelines, so officials have an unobstructed view of the out-of-bounds area.

(Above) Players from Duke University (striped helmets) and University of Southern California clash in Rose Bowl game in pre-World War II days. Note the eyebrow tackle against the ball carrier—no face masks in those days. Data: 4" × 5" Speed Graphic, 135mm lens, 1/550 sec. at f/5.6, Kodak Super Panchro-Press Type B. Photo by Don Downie.

(Right) Although obsolete by modern photographic standards, 4" × 5" press cameras are useful for special situations where a large-format negative or transparency is required. A Speed Graphic was used for this action shot at Pittsburgh Steelers-Los Angeles Rams game to meet a client's request for a wall-sized mural. Data: 4" × 5" Speed Graphic, 240mm lens, 1/1000 sec. at f/8, Kodak Super Panchro-Press Type B.

2. Don't get between the poles of the 10-yard marker chain held by the field linesmen to measure first downs. If they have to move back quickly, you may get tripped.

3. Keep down when at the sidelines so you don't block the spectator's view of the game. This can be very hard on the knees, but it is necessary. Some photographers tape small rubber sponges to each knee to ease the pain of kneeling for long periods.

Pick the side of the field that offers the best light. Avoid shooting into the sun unless you are seeking silhouette effects. Determine your exposure in advance. You won't have time to fumble with shutter speeds and lens apertures when the action gets underway. The camera should be prefocused before a play begins. Unless you are equipped with a long focal-length lens, wait until the action moves in close before tripping the shutter. With a normal lens, set the focus at 25 or 30 feet and wait until the players are within range. Be patient, and let the action come to you! Otherwise, negative images will be too small to enlarge well.

If you want to pick off action shots at mid-field you'll need telephoto lenses, upward of 85mm on 35mm equipment. The 100–200mm focal lengths are ideal for shooting from the sidelines and are widely used by

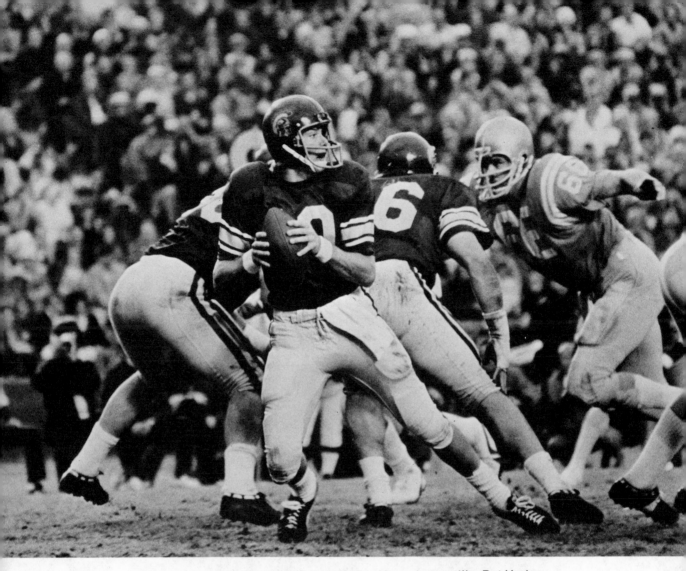

Long lenses can be used to pull in shots of key players, like Pat Haden, USC's quarterback, in action against U.C.L.A. Data: motorized Nikon, 300mm lens, 1/500 sec. at f/5.6, Tri-X rated at ASA 800, dark, cloudy day with stadium lights on, developed in Acufine.

professionals. In the 2¹/₄″ format, lenses of 150mm and longer are preferred. They allow a greater choice of pictures since it is possible to photograph plays at a considerable distance and still get a negative image that will stand tremendous enlargement.

Use of extra-long telephoto lenses (300–400mm) allows an even greater selection of pictures. You can reach out into the far corners of the field to grab a closeup of a key player or a choice burst of action like a fumble or pass interception. They are great for color where you must do most of your cropping in the camera rather than the darkroom, and they make it easy to shoot frame-filling transparencies.

Plate 1. Players scramble to recover fumbled ball during UCLA intra-squad exhibition game. Data: motorized Nikon, 135mm lens, 1/500 sec. at f/5.6 on Kodachrome 64 film.

Plate 2. Sunlight reflecting through blades of wide-angle lens diaphragm at small aperture produced this interesting star-burst effect in photo of skiers riding chair lift at Bear Valley, California. This effect is simple to obtain when shooting into sun that is low on the horizon—late afternoon or very early morning. Data: Miranda, 35mm lens, 1/250 sec. at f/16 on Ektachrome-X film. Photo by Elmar Baxter.

Plate 3. Outboard race driver Dick Sherrer, photographed with remote-control motorized camera mounted on his boat during a practice run in the Outboard World Championship at Lake Havasu, Arizona. Data: motorized Nikon, 8mm fisheye lens, 1/500 sec. at *f*/8 on Ektachrome-X film.

Plate 4. Panning the camera at a slow shutter speed produced graphic blurred-action view of night football game. Data: Nikon, 180mm lens, 1/15 sec. at f/8 on High Speed Ektachrome Tungsten (Type B) film, available light. Photo by Sheedy & Long.

Plate 5. With fast lenses and high-speed color films, it is possible to photograph sports action indoors by available light. Los Angeles Lakers –Golden State Warriors basketball game was covered from sidelines. Data: motorized Nikon, 50mm lens, 1/250 sec. at f/2 on High Speed Ektachrome Tungsten (Type B) film, rated at ASA 320 and pushed 1½ stops in processing.

Plate 6. A skier bends into a turn in downhill slalom course during Olympic trials at Squaw Valley, California. Data: motorized Nikon, 300mm lens, 1/500 sec. at f/8 on Ektachrome-X film. Photo by Sheedy & Long.

Plate 7. Chris Evert (background), ranked No. 1 among women pros, teams up with Billie Jean King, ranked No. 2, in doubles match. Data: Minolta, 100mm lens, 1/500 sec. at f/6.3 on Ektachrome-X film.

Plate 8. High jumper spoils the jump as he hits the bar. Data: Minolta, 35mm lens, 1/500 sec. at f/4.5 on Kodachrome II film. Plate 9. Champion water skier Ricky McCormick competes in water-ski tournament at Holiday Island, Arkansas. At left is Christy Freeman, a former women's champion, who competed in the trick-skiing doubles event with Ricky. Data: motorized Nikon, 105mm lens, 1/1000 sec. at f/6.3 on Ektachrome-X film, rated at ASA 125 and pushed 1 stop in processing.

Plate 10. Panning the camera at a fast shutter speed made it possible to get sharp photo of Lloyd Ruby's Eagle-Offy racer traveling at 180 miles per hour in California 500. Data: Nikon, 300mm lens, 1/500 sec. at f/5.6 on Ektachrome-X film.

Plate 11. Thoroughbred racing at Hollywood Park, California, with straight-on view from camera position near outside rail. Data: motorized Nikon, 85–250mm zoom lens, 1/500 sec. at f/8 on High Speed Ektachrome Daylight film. Photo by Vic Stein.

(Right) Archie Manning, New Orleans Saints' quarterback, could not escape Los Angeles Rams' defensive ends Fred Dryer, tackling him from below, and Jack Youngblood, leaping high at right. Manning lost 13 yards on this play, one of several broken up by powerful Rams' defense as they beat the Saints 27-13 at Los Angeles Coliseum. Data: Nikon, 80-200mm zoom lens, 1/1000 sec. at f/8, Tri-X.

(Below) Fast telephoto lenses make it possible to cover mid-field football action from the sidelines under existing-light conditions. A key block by U.C.L.A.'s fullback Ray Smith (21) cut down Purdue's defensive back Robert Jarus (43), enabling the ball carrier, halfback Bob Smith, to break loose for a touchdown. Data: Nikon, 105mm lens, 1/500 sec. at f/2.8, Tri-X rated at ASA 1200, developed in Ethol UFG.

(Above) Frank Gifford, New York Giants' running back, makes a mighty effort but can't quite reach the ball in game with the Los Angeles Rams. Defending on the play are Rams' linebackers Ed Meador (21) and Bill Jobko (57). Photo was an award-winner in Popular Photography International Picture Contest. Data: Nikon, 105mm lens, 1/500 sec. at f/2.8, Agfa Isopan Record film rated at ASA 1600, available light in football stadium, PRA developer, Photo courtesy of Ziff-Davis Publishing Company.

(Left) Don Paul, Los Angeles Rams' assistant coach, appears worried as he listens to reports on his field telephone about the movement of the opposing team from observers high in the press box. The coach and reserve players sweating out the game on the sidelines are always good subjects. Data: Nikon, 105mm lens, 1/250 sec. at f/5.6, Tri-X, overcast day.

Chief drawback of the big telephotos is their comparatively shallow depth of field, especially at wide apertures. Focusing must be critical. If properly used, however, these lenses will secure many excellent pictures that would be completely impossible to get otherwise. Their limited depth of field can even be made to work for you by isolating the subject against an out-of-focus background, thereby eliminating distracting elements and strengthening the picture. With fast (ASA 400) black-and-white films, you are frequently shooting with an aperture of $f/8$–$f/16$ in brilliant sunshine, even at shutter speeds of $1/500$ sec. or $1/1000$ sec. This may create a condition where you actually have too much depth of field! The stadium backgrounds are needle sharp with spectators, cheerleaders, and reserve players on the far sidelines popping out in the wrong places. Very long lenses will help in eliminating these defects. An alternative to an extra-bright lighting situation is to use a slower film, or a neutral-density filter to reduce the speed of a fast film.

Follow the teams up the sidelines, staying a few yards ahead of the line of scrimmage. When the players head your way, wait until you have a clear shot at the ball carrier before making the picture. That pigskin he's carrying is the center of interest. Don't waste film where it is not visible because such pictures are meaningless unless there is unusual side action involved in the scene. Two examples would be a lineman sent sprawling by a vicious block or a defensive back poised to knock down a pass.

When the team with the ball is deep inside its opponent's territory, position yourself behind the end zone to be ready for a potential touchdown play. Keep alert, move in the direction of the play after the ball is snapped, and try to catch the ball carrier plunging over the goal line to score. If there is an end run or a pass to a receiver in the corner of the end zone, you will have to move swiftly in order to get the picture.

Fast exposures are essential in football photography. To insure stopping rapid motion from just about any camera angle, you'll need at least $1/500$ sec. However, if your shutter is limited to $1/200$ sec. or $1/250$ sec., it is possible to achieve good results by timing the exposure for when the players are coming directly at the camera. You can do this by remaining about 10 yards ahead of the line of scrimmage. From this position, the action on your side will nearly always be head-on, or close to a 45-degree angle, thus reducing the possibility of blurred images. This is handy to remember in low-light situations, when you are forced to shoot at slower shutter speeds. As a general rule, always shoot as fast as your shutter and the available light will permit.

Don't forget to watch for good human-interest shots when you are on the sidelines. Candid studies of players on the bench watching their teammates in action as well as of the cheerleaders and the yelling fans in the grandstands are welcome additions to your game coverage and present football from a different point of view. Try shooting the opposing coaches, platoons of players during the pregame warmup, the bands at halftime, and other details that capture the spirit and emotion of football.

SOCCER AND RUGBY

The same principles used to cover football may be applied to soccer and rugby. Soccer is the original version of football. It was played in England as far back as 100 A.D. and is probably the world's most popular sport. Attendance at major soccer matches in Europe and South America is often greater than the enormous crowds at the annual football bowl games played each New Year's Day in the United States.

Soccer is an exciting game to photograph with play going on continuously. There are no downs as in football, where the action is momentarily halted as the teams line up to face each other. Like American football, soccer is played by 2 teams of 11 men each. The soccer ball is round, instead of elliptical, and slightly smaller than a regulation basketball. Scoring is one point for each goal, as in hockey. A player may advance the ball by kicking or butting it with his head and shoulders. No player, except the goalie in a defensive effort to prevent a score, may use his hands or arms to move the ball. Passing the ball forward or laterally is forbidden. If a player other than the goalie handles the ball manually, a penalty is called against him, and the opposing team is awarded a free kick that can mean a score and a good photo.

Soccer players dress in shorts, unpadded jerseys, heavy stockings, shin guards, and shoes with blocked leather tips for booting the ball. Crunching body contact often takes place when defensive players try to kick the ball away from an opponent advancing on their goal. As in football, there is heavy action in the goal area when the offensive team is in scoring position.

While the popularity of soccer in the United States has not been high, it is growing steadily. Many high schools and colleges now include soccer in their sports programs, and professional soccer is gaining

Douglas McMillian of Los Angeles Aztecs' pro soccer team takes a tumble after preventing ball from going out of bounds in game with the Seattle Sounders. Soccer offers the sports photographer a variety of exciting action shots comparable to football. Data: motorized Nikon, 105mm lens, 1/500 sec. at f/16, Tri-X. Photo by Bill Varie, *Los Angeles Times.*

(Right) Brazilian goalkeeper Leao and defenseman Ulibari block attack by Poland's Szarmach, at center, during 1974 World Cup soccer competition. Data: 35mm camera, telephoto lens, fast pan film. Wide World photo.

(Below) Rugby is a bruising contact sport that combines elements of both football and soccer. The players do not wear helmets or any protective padding. In this photo, two tacklers bring down the ball carrier in an amateur rugby league game. Data: Nikon, 200mm lens, 1/1000 sec. at f/11, Tri-X. Photo by Keith Rodabaugh.

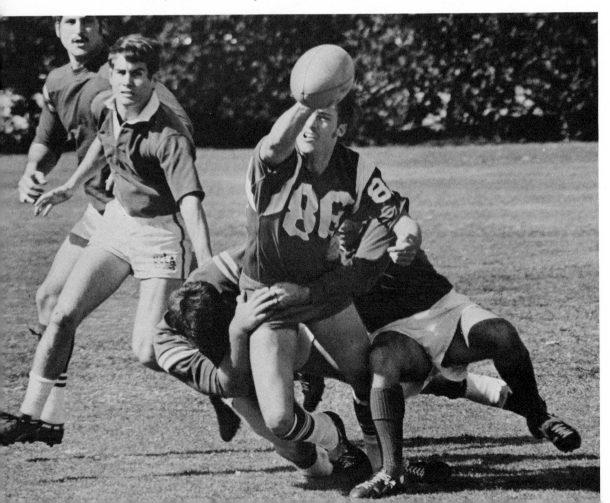

Players collide as they leap for a pass in amateur rugby league game.
Data: Nikon, 200mm lens, 1/1000 sec. at f/11, Tri-X. Photo by Keith
Rodabaugh.

Two opposing rugby teams collide in rugged scrimmage during amateur league game. Data: Nikon, 200mm lens, 1/1000 sec. at f/11, Tri-X. Photo by Keith Rodabaugh.

strength with active teams in several large cities competing against each other on a regular schedule.

Rugby is also a football-type game, named after the renowned English public school where it originated in the early 1800's. While soccer permits the movement of the ball only by kicking or butting with head and shoulders, rugby introduced the idea of a player carrying the ball as well. Passing the ball laterally or to the rear is acceptable, but a forward pass to a teammate is not allowed. Tackling and blocking are also permitted, but unlike American football, there can be no blocking in advance of the ball carrier. Another feature of rugby allows a ball rolling on the ground to be kicked.

Rugby is a far more strenuous game than football. Players wear no helmets or protective padding, and there are no time-outs or substitutions. If a player appears to be badly injured, the referee may halt the game at his discretion.

Although popular in some colleges, rugby in the United States has been almost totally eclipsed by football. Throughout the British Commonwealth, however, rugby has a tremendous following, particularly in Australia and New Zealand.

CHAPTER 10

GOLF

A golf tournament is probably the biggest challenge to a sports photographer. It is a subject with many built-in restrictions that make it very difficult to cover.

Professional Golf Association tournaments simply will not permit photographers without press credentials, and in fact, they prohibit spectators from bringing a camera to the course. The reason is that dozens of shutters, clicking indiscriminately, distract the pro-golfers, who are a notoriously touchy bunch in such a high-pressure, big-money sport.

The nonaccredited photographer stands a much better chance at his local country club, public golf course, or charity and celebrity events where restrictions against cameras may be relaxed. Top-ranked golfers also play exhibition games or participate in mixed professional–amateur tournaments where photographers are welcomed.

The prime rule in shooting golf is to stay out of the golfer's line of sight. This is a sport requiring the utmost concentration, and even the faintest distraction is intolerable. Never shoot when the golfer is lining up a stroke—driving off a tee, shooting on the fairway (an approach to a green), or putting. The sound of the shutter may affect his timing and cause a miss. A motorized camera is especially nerve-jarring to a golfer, sounding more like a heavy-caliber machine gun.

The longer the lens, the less conspicuous you are, and the more efficiently you can function. The 200–400mm telephotos are strongly recommended for tournament coverage, with some photographers favoring even longer optics, up to 600mm. For the informal atmosphere of

exhibitions or most amateur events, you can get by with much shorter focal lengths.

Golfers' faces are usually heavily shaded by their peaked caps and hats, making it difficult to get good expressions. Take advantage of situations where the golfer's face is visible. It is the normal reaction for the golfer to look up after hitting a ball to follow its flight. That's the moment to shoot. If you can show the ball somewhere in the picture area, so much the better. A shot like this requires flawless timing and

(Left) Spectators watch golfers on green during tournament at Palm Springs, California. Rugged mountains in background add interest to the picture, shot from the side of a hill. Data: Nikon, 28mm lens, 1/125 sec. at f/8. Black-and-white print from Kodachrome II transparency. Photo by Sheedy and Long.

(Below) Photograph of professional golfer Jack Nicklaus and his caddie in action at the 1966 Masters Tournament at Augusta, Georgia. Data: 35mm camera, telephoto lens, Tri-X. Photo by Fred W. Lyon, UPI.

A golfer knocks the ball out of a sand trap at Pebble Beach, California, golf course. A camera angle was selected to show the ball on its way to the green with the flag marking the hole in the foreground. Data: Nikon, 200mm lens, 1/500 sec. at f/4. Black-and-white print from Kodachrome II transparency. Photo by Sheedy and Long.

considerable luck. A low camera angle may be advisable to secure a stronger visual effect. It may also help in eliminating a distracting background of trees and foliage.

Follow the players along the course, keeping alert for small details that can be helpful. A left-handed player will always start his swing with the club over his left shoulder. To show his face in a side view, you must be on his left and at an angle, otherwise it may be hidden as he connects with the ball. Conversely, right-handed players must be covered from the right side. An exception to this rule is if you are working at a great distance with a very long lens, well out in front of the golfer, but off to one side where you are out of his direct vision. Keep an eye on the flight of the ball. A badly directed swing may send it streaking your way. Always be prepared to duck.

Sand traps are located at various points along the course, especially near the greens in order to catch the player who makes mistakes. They are hated by golfers but liked by photographers because of the splendid explosion of sand that occurs when the golfer attempts to blast the ball loose. The sand acts as a natural reflector to illuminate the golfer's face.

Once the ball is on the green, the player attempts to sink the ball into the cup with his putter. This is often worth a picture because of the agonized or joyful reactions that take place if he misses the putt or makes it. Remember to stay out of his line of sight, and don't move

A pair of deer calmly strolls across the fairway at Pebble Beach, California, championship golf course while player in background lines up his shot. Data: Nikon, 300mm lens, 1/500 sec. at f/4. Black-and-white print from Kodachrome II transparency. Photo by Sheedy and Long.

around or talk when he is lining up the putt. In working around a green, look for an angle where you can cover the approach and putt from the same position.

Water holes are the golfer's nemesis and can provide a great many human-interest pictures. Watch for intense facial expressions as the player attempts to hit the ball across the water. Anxious eyes follow its flight, hoping to avoid seeing the splash that signifies a lost ball and a one-stroke penalty. The combination of a classic golfing position, with the club poised over a shoulder, and a strained expression usually makes a good shot.

If you are after closeups of individual golfers, it may be possible to get them on the practice tee before a match. Here the photographer has much greater freedom of movement, working at closer distances than is possible out on the course. Experiment with different lenses and camera positions to get what you need. Virtually all golf courses will let you work on the practice tee as long as you don't interfere with the players warming up.

Golfer lining up a putt is a study in absolute concentration. A camera angle was chosen to show another golfer in the foreground for added interest. A long telephoto lens tied all the elements together for an appealing picture. Data: motorized Nikon, 400mm lens, 1/250 sec. at f/6.3. Black-and-white print from Kodachrome II transparency. Photo by Sheedy and Long.

CHAPTER 11

HOCKEY

Hockey is played at a lightning pace, but it is not a particularly troublesome indoor sport to the photographer who is able to pick the moments of peak action.

Despite the rapid play, there are a great many moments of apparent action when the players are not really moving fast. The face-off at the start of the game is an example. For the face-off, the centers of both teams confront each other in the middle of the ice, and the referee tosses the puck between them. The battle is then on. But watch closely; just before the puck hits the ice, the athletes are tensed in a low crouch, sticks poised for a quick thrust. Their strained faces mirror a determination that can make an exceptional picture. This scene can easily be recorded at a moderate shutter speed of $1/125$ sec. or even $1/60$ sec.

As the puck drops, the two players lunge to meet it. One man is a shade faster than his rival and whacks the puck down the ice to a teammate. He, in turn, fields it with his hockey stick while skating toward the opposing team's goal. But a defending guard slides out to meet him, blocking his path. The man with the puck skids to a halt amid a flying spray of ice. He searches anxiously for an unguarded companion to receive a pass. Here again, you have it: tense, strained athletes poised for swift movement. The defending player slashes at the puck, batting it free, and the other team moves to the attack. The identical thrust and parry routine is repeated as the players maneuver down the ice.

Now the game is in high gear. Several defending players converge on the man with the puck as he veers closer to the goal line. At last he's

In this series, Los Angeles Kings' (light uniforms) and Vancouver Canucks' players battle for loose puck in front of Kings' goal. This is an example of hockey action that could be shot by an amateur photographer from a balcony seat in the arena with a clear view of the ice. In this case, the photographer was in the third row of seats, shooting over the heads of fans in front of him. A first-row seat would have been better, but these are sometimes hard to get at a popular sports attraction. Data: Minolta, 135mm lens, 1/500 sec. at f/2.8, Tri-X rated at ASA 1000, available light, developed in Acufine.

in range, deftly feinting to maneuver the last guard out of position. He draws back the stick and slams the puck—that's one picture. He follows through—another picture. The goalie, down on his knees in front of the net, neatly blocks the shot with his stick—a really good picture if you time it right.

Les Coldwill, Vancouver Canucks' forward, slams the puck past New York Rangers' goalie Lorne Worsley to score the game-tying point. John Hanna, Rangers' defenseman, could not stop Coldwill's perfectly executed shot from point-blank range. However, brilliant effort by Coldwill was not enough to prevent a strong Rangers team from fighting back to win 3-2 in NHL hockey game at Los Angeles, California. Data: Nikon, 105mm lens, 1/500 sec. at f/2.8, Tri-X rated at ASA 1000, developed in Ethol UFG.

This action can be stopped with a shutter speed of $^1/_{250}$ sec. or $^1/_{500}$ sec. although the puck may be blurred at the slower speed.

The puck, having been deflected by the goalie, is taken over by the goalie's teammates, and the whole attack-defense process is renewed.

Photographing hockey games, therefore, becomes a classic study in anticipating the action and shooting the picture at the instant of arrested motion. The face-off can be photographed from almost any position, but it is easier if you are situated opposite the center of the ice. Face-offs also take place at other locations during a game. They occur when several players are locked in close contact while trying to gain possession of the puck. When a situation arises where nobody can move, the referee halts the play, and a new face-off is held to get the puck into motion.

A central location is excellent for covering the back-and-forth maneuvering of the teams. Establish a point of focus about 25 feet out from the sidelines, and then work in a semi-circular sweep on both sides of your position. If the action suddenly moves in close, you'll have to change focus quickly to get the shot.

Action at the goals is best captured from the side of the ice in line with the net or slightly to either side. You'll have a good choice of angles to show the goalie trying to intercept the puck and prevent a score. Watch for bruising physical contact as opposing players body check, use of one's body as a weapon, each other. Medium telephoto lenses of 85–135mm are ideal.

The lighting in most pro hockey arenas permits fast exposures of $^1/_{250}$ sec. or $^1/_{500}$ sec. at $f/2.8$ on fast pan film rated at ASA 800 or higher. You gain an added bonus from light reflected off the surface of the ice, which helps to fill in shadow areas. Like a boxing arena, powerful interior illumination can lead your meter astray. Don't be fooled by inflated readings. Base proper exposure on the faces of the hockey players.

Some amateur and semipro teams play in makeshift arenas with very poor lighting. In those arenas you'll need a strobe to work effectively.

Other aspects of hockey, such as substitute players intently watching the game from the bench, referees on skates along the side of the rink, the partisan crowd cheering the home team, are all good subject material for a picture story.

CHAPTER 12

TENNIS

Tennis is another popular sport that provides top-notch action subjects. At most amateur and interscholastic matches, you are free to move around the perimeter of the court without restrictions. A normal lens or medium telephoto is excellent for most pictures, depending on your location. Big-time professional tennis requires the customary press credentials to gain entry; photographers may have to work at a greater distance from designated positions, which requires longer lenses.

Although the game is played at a rapid pace, there are those instances of arrested motion that are easy to shoot—a player at the beginning of his serve as he throws the ball up in the air or a player with his racket poised to return his opponent's stroke. Serving is always done from the rear of the court, and focusing is a simple matter.

After the serve is completed, the action speeds up as the players rally the ball back and forth across the net. It is rather difficult to establish a definite spot on which to focus because the players are constantly changing position. You will probably get the most satisfactory results by prefocusing on a point in the middle of the court and letting the depth of field of your lens work for you.

Watch the game carefully, and as a player approaches the point of focus, commence shooting. If you've done your homework well and know the approximate depth of field of a lens at a specific aperture, chances are good that nearly all your pictures will be sharp.

As you become adept at photographing tennis, you'll recognize the different playing patterns of each competitor. One player may rush the net after every serve, hoping to be in position to smash back his oppo-

Ruling queen of the Women's Pro Tennis Tour Billie Jean King concentrates on the ball as she runs to return a shot by Rosemary Casals in the Virginia Slims Tournament. Data: Minolta, 400mm lens, 1/1000 sec. at f/11, Tri-X. Camera was positioned at top of tennis stadium and used with monopod for added steadiness.

A fierce competitor on the Women's Pro Tour, Rosemary Casals seldom wins a match against top-ranked Billie Jean King, but she keeps trying. The following series of pictures was made at the Virginia Slims Tournament at Mission Viejo, Los Angeles, California. They emphasize Miss Casals' grim determination to someday dethrone the champ. All photos were shot from the sidelines of the court. (1) Rosemary Casals tensely waits to receive the serve from Billie Jean King. (2) She advances to hit the ball. (3) Rosemary addresses the ball for a forehand return.

(4) Aggressively, Rosemary returns a hard-hit shot by Billie Jean. (5) Following through on her return, Rosemary eyes the ball in flight. (6) Disgusted, she kicks at ball after missing a shot. Data: motorized Minolta, 200mm lens, 1/1000 sec. at f/8, Tri-X.

nent's return. Another player may hug the baseline, aiming his return shots to the far corner of the opposite court where it will be difficult for his rival to reach.

Should a player exhibit a particular weakness, like a poor backhand stroke, you can bet his opponent will hit every ball possible to a position where a backhand is required. Any tennis player who hits a high lob, the equivalent of a slow pop fly in baseball, had better be prepared to receive a scorching overhead smash from across the net.

A good way to cover tennis is to work along the perimeter of the court for the first few games, then go up in the stands for a high viewpoint. Get some representative views of the entire court showing both players, then switch to a longer lens and dramatize one contestant. Aim for moments when his face is contorted with tension as he prepares to slam the ball. With a 200mm or 300mm lens, you may find an angle that will show both players at once. This kind of shot usually requires a camera position facing the rear of the court, looking toward the net. It is also effective for pictures of doubles matches, with two players on each side. A high viewpoint also simplifies the background because you are shooting down at the players, avoiding the crowd, fencing, and other distracting elements.

To show the player's racket at the moment of impact with the ball, a minimum shutter speed of $1/500$ sec. is suggested, and even then the ball may be somewhat blurred. At $1/1000$ sec. all but the fastest motion will be stopped. If you are limited to a slower speed like $1/250$ sec. because of poor light, time the exposure for the instant when the player's racket is poised to strike, just before he starts his swing. You'll be surprised how quickly you learn to gauge the peak of action.

For many years, white was the standard color of tennis uniforms. Nowadays, the brighter pastel shades are gaining popularity, making it a lot easier to secure interesting color transparencies.

Many tennis players wear small caps to shade their eyes during a match. These hats cause troublesome shadows that make it difficult to show faces. A low camera angle from the side of the court will help to overcome this defect. On some courts, reflected light from the sun gives a slight fill-in from below that may show facial detail. This fill-in depends on the color of the material used to surface the court, and you should not count on it.

For off-beat pictures of tournament tennis, watch the players as they leave the court after finishing the first set. If it has been a difficult battle, their faces may register strained expressions of fatigue. With a telephoto lens, you can stand at a discreet distance and show them at rest, trying to regain strength for the next round of play.

Margaret Court reaches to backhand a shot during the first "Tennis Battle of the Sexes" challenge match with 55-year-old Bobby Riggs. Mrs. Court lost the match to Riggs, a former world-champion tennis star in the 1940's. Data: motorized Nikon, 300mm lens, 1/500 sec. at f/16, Tri-X. Camera angle was selected to utilize telephoto lens in order to pull in both players in a tight composition. Photo by Bob Flora, UPI.

CHAPTER 13

TRACK MEETS

The track meet offers a variety of dramatic action pictures. The speeding sprinters racing the split second of a timer's stopwatch, the graceful leap of a pole vaulter etched against the sky—these are only a few of the excellent picture possibilities to be found at any track meet.

There are very few restrictions placed on photographers working at an outdoor meet. The main requirement is that you stay off the track while a race is in progress and also out of the path of contestants performing in various field events—pole vault, high jump, and others. The beginning or end of a race can be photographed from the side of the track. You may also take a position at any point between the start and finish lines, providing you don't block the vision of judges or timers. Because it is usually possible to work very close to the track, normal or wide-angle lenses may be used to good advantage.

Indoor meets frequently have more restrictions placed on photographers due to the limited amount of space. Only press and magazine photographers with proper credentials are permitted to work along the perimeter of the track. Amateur or other nonaccredited cameramen must get their pictures from seats within the spectators' area. Telephoto lenses are very helpful under these conditions.

Covering a track meet calls for a certain routine. Hurdle events are shot at the initial barrier just in front of the start line. The athletes are pretty well bunched at that point, and it is possible to show all the entries. After the first hurdle, they are usually spread out as the faster runners move in front. The same principle applies to distance events like the mile run. Get the runners on the first lap if you wish to show

To show all the runners in a 120-yard high hurdles race at a Los Angeles Valley Junior College-San Diego Marines track meet, a camera position at the first hurdle was selected. At any point further along the track, the runners might have been spread out too far for a good picture. Data: Nikon, 35mm lens, 1/1000 sec. at f/5.6, Tri-X, cloudy day.

them all together. However, if you are interested in showing only the winners of these races, then pick a location near the last hurdle or the finish line.

Track meets are ideally suited for the panning technique. During a sprint event like the 100- or 220-yard run, move the camera smoothly and steadily to keep the athletes centered in your viewfinder. As they run in front, trip the shutter, but keep the camera moving in a follow-through motion as they pass. A shutter speed as low as 1/125 sec. will stop most of the action against a streaky, blurred background, suggesting great speed. A slower speed like 1/30 sec. or 1/60 sec. will further blur the arms and legs and make the runners appear to be racing at 100 miles per hour. Be careful, though, these slower speeds are dangerous

(Above) Paul Underwood, Arizona State University high jumper, clears bar at 7'3" to finish second behind Dwight Stones at Los Angeles Sports Arena Indoor Track Meet. Underwood eyes a soft landing spot as he plunges downward. Data: Nikon, 50mm lens, 1/500 sec. at f/2.8, Tri-X rated at ASA 1000, developed in Acufine.

(Left) Barry Brown, Florida Track Club, leads the field in 2-mile run at Los Angeles Sports Arena Indoor Track Meet. A wide aperture and selective focus were utilized to concentrate on Brown at the request of a client. Data: Nikon, 105mm lens, 1/500 sec. at f/2.8, Tri-X rated at ASA 1000, available light, developed in Acufine.

(Above) Dwight Stones, 20, Pacific Coast Track Club, clears the bar at 7'4¼" for a new U.S. indoor record at Los Angeles Sports Arena Track Meet. Photo was made at the peak of action just as Stones reached the highest point of his jump. Data: motorized Minolta, 35mm lens, 1/500 sec. at f/2.8, Tri-X rated at ASA 1000, developed in Acufine.

(Right) The start of a sprint event in a track meet offers many exciting shots. Runners break from starting blocks that are staggered to equalize running distance around an oval track. Data: Rolleiflex, 80mm lens, 1/250 sec. at f/16, Tri-X. The camera was placed on the ground next to contestant at right.

to use unless you're well versed in panning. There is too much danger of jerking the camera and ruining the picture.

If you prefer your action frozen, the higher shutter speeds are essential. A minimum of $1/500$ sec. or $1/1000$ sec. is necessary to stop the fast-moving hurdle races, sprint events, and relays. The pole vault and high jump can safely be covered at slower speeds like $1/250$ sec., if you're able to time the exposure for the peak of action as the contestant clears the bar. He will be suspended in mid-air for a fraction of a second before plunging downward.

Relay races are interesting events. You can station yourself either along the track, to catch the runners passing their batons to teammates, or at the finish line. In a long race like the half- or one-mile relays, there will be several groups of contestants alternating for opposing teams and offering plenty of chances to shoot. Each group of runners may take several laps. It is wise, therefore, to check with officials beforehand to get the approximate locations where the athletes exchange batons.

Outdoor night events or indoor meets can usually be photographed by existing light with fast lenses and film. Here again, the panning technique can help in producing sharp action pictures even at the low light levels that normally exist under these conditions.

If light levels are inadequate, then a strobe light will be required for best results. Open up your lens at least one full stop over the normal exposure to compensate for the lack of light-reflecting surfaces.

There is room for originality in photographing track meets. The standard shot for a long time has been the runners breaking through

the tape at the finish line. While this dramatic moment is necessary in race coverage, don't neglect the beginning of an event. You can make some exciting shots just as the runners break from the starting line or as they round the half-way point along the track. Working from the inside of a turn may also provide good camera angles. The tense facial expressions of the runners as they negotiate the curve can make an interesting shot.

When you are covering a meet for publication, field events like the high jump can be a problem if there are many competitors. It is next to impossible to pick a winner from the 20 or more entries. Keep an eye on the scores as they are recorded or announced over the public address system. This way you can narrow down the field to the top three or four jumpers and avoid wasting a lot of time and film. Sometimes the winner of an event will oblige photographers with a few exhibition jumps if he is not too tired. However, athletes can be pretty temperamental, and it is best not to depend on this occurrence. Try to get at least one shot during the actual event to protect yourself. Watch that camera angle to avoid having an arm or shoulder cover the athlete's face.

Track meets are fun to shoot and offer a real challenge to your ability to handle fast action.

Runner in a steeplechase event sends a shower of spray flying as he charges through a water hole. Available light at a night track meet offered a chance to record an impressionistic view of the event rather than clearly defined action. Both approaches have their place in sports photography. Data: motorized Nikon, 105mm lens, 1/250 sec. at f/2.8, Tri-X rated at ASA 1600. Photo by Ernie Schworck, UPI.

CHAPTER 14

MOTOR SPORTS

AUTOMOBILE SPEEDWAY RACING

Auto racing is an incredibly exciting sport that challenges a photographer to match his shooting skills against powerful super-machines traveling at speeds up to 200 miles per hour. Besides vivid action, the carnival atmosphere of a motor speedway on race day also presents a lively array of feature pictures.

Caravans of campers, vans, and cars filled with spectators jam every available space. In the garages and pit area, sleek racers, painted in bold colors, are finely tuned by mechanics, clad in white, as their drivers watch vigilantly. A visitor is conscious of the underlying tone of tension and fear, the undefinable odors of oil and fresh rubber, and the deafening symphony of many engines warming up at once.

The amateur photographer has a better chance for a truly spectacular picture at an auto race than at most other professional sports. In baseball or football, he is seldom allowed to get close enough to the play. However, a motor speedway is huge, and just about any point on the track can be a scene of wild action. The pro photographer covering a race can't be at the right spot all the time. For the amateur, shooting from the stands can produce an exclusive series of pictures if there is a wreck or some other unusual incident within range.

Most tracks are designed to give the fans a good view of the action, and many excellent shots have been taken by amateurs from outside the perimeter fence. Local newspapers and the wire services are always interested in dramatic action or crash pictures and may buy yours if their staff photographers were not at the scene.

A 200–300mm telephoto lens is a must for working at the distances

(Above) McLaren-Offy race car is rolled from garage area before start of California 500 auto race at Ontario Motor Speedway. Front cowling of car has not been put in place at this point. Data: Nikon, 28mm lens, 1/250 sec. at f/11, Tri-X, overcast day.

(Below) Start of the California 500 auto race at Ontario Motor Speedway. To show all the entries in an auto race, it is best to catch them right at the beginning. After the race starts, the racers become strung out as the faster ones move ahead, making it difficult to get a good picture. Data: motorized Nikon, 200mm lens, 1/500 sec. at f/11, Tri-X.

Race car driver Rex Mays hurtles to his death in a crash at the Del Mar, California, track. Note the shattered fence posts flying through the air at right. This photo won top prize in Graflex Corporation Sports Photo Contest and was widely used in newspapers throughout the United States. Data: 4″ × 5″ Speed Graphic, 10-inch 250mm telephoto lens, 1/1000 sec. at f/8, Kodak Super Panchro-Press Type B. Photo supplied by Don Downie, courtesy of Graflex Corporation.

normally encountered. Every track is different, and at some a 135mm telephoto is long enough for many pictures. But in other instances, lenses as long as 400mm or 500mm will be needed for the best possible results.

Even if you have access to a closer track-side location, it is a good idea to remain at least 100–150 feet away. This is not only for safety's sake, but also because the eye commands a greater field of view at that distance, making it easier to follow action.

Experienced racing cameramen like to take a position near a turn since crack-ups are most likely to happen there. Track officials may cut small holes in the fence or erect special platforms to accommodate photographers. Virtually all tracks require credentials for admittance to these preferred locations.

The photographer of motor sports must be adept at panning. Even $1/1000$ sec. won't stop a race car speeding at 180 miles per hour. With proper panning technique, $1/500$ sec. or even $1/250$ sec. will work beautifully.

For some really far-out, blurred images, shoot at speeds from $1/30$–$1/125$ sec. while you pan the camera with the car. If you have a zoom lens, try panning the camera and zooming the lens at the same time. The results are unpredictable, and you might waste a lot of film. However, just one startling picture that conveys a feeling of explosive speed will make it all worthwhile.

Depending on how serious you are, you may want to visit the speedway a few days before the event and scout around for good shooting positions. The drivers may be taking practice runs, and officials may be more inclined to be lenient about admitting you to areas that are closed to fans during the actual race.

It may even be possible to enter the garages and pit area for close-ups of individual cars and drivers. If it's portraits you're after, you must get there at the right time—just before a driver puts on his headgear. Once the helmet, visor, and dust mask are in place, a driver's face is hidden.

Often, short preliminary races are held to qualify drivers for starting positions in the main event. This is a good time to practice your panning technique under race conditions and to get accustomed to the fantastic speeds.

Be sure to bring ear plugs or cotton to protect your hearing because the noise level close to the track is deafening. Also, pack a supply of plastic bags for your equipment and a raincoat for you in case the weather turns sour. Every lens should be fitted with a Skylight or UV filter to protect it from fine dust and flying gravel that are present at all tracks.

On race day, plan to arrive at the track at least three hours before the start. Crowds build up rapidly, and you might find spectators blocking some good camera angles you had scouted earlier.

Most speedways are laid out in an oval, but many include interior road racecourses with tricky S-turns, hills, and other obstacles designed to test a driver's skill to the utmost. You should be able to find at least one good shooting location on nearly every turn and straightaway.

A parade lap precedes the official start. This is a good time to shoot

Motorcycle racer becomes airborne as he bounces over the crest of a hill in rugged motocross event. Data: Hasselblad, 250mm lens, 1/500 sec. at f/11, Tri-X. Photo by Steve Reyes, *Popular Cycling Magazine.*

the racers moving down the track behind the pace car. They will not be traveling quite as fast as they do after the green flag drops and the race begins.

When you are close to the track at ground level, the most important thing to remember is *never turn your back on the cars.* Spinouts and crashes can happen anywhere on the course, at any time. An out-of-control racer may smash through the perimeter fence near your position. Always be prepared to run. It could save your life.

Track the racers as they speed across your field of view, and release the shutter when they reach your prefocused point. You'll find that cars of the same class generally maintain the same speed every time they pass a given point on a turn or straightaway. This consistency helps in anticipating a picture when you are working from that location.

As the race nears its end, try to station yourself to show the lead cars crossing the finish line. This is not easy to accomplish at a major race where nonaccredited photographers are barred from all the good locations. Your best bet is to work with a long lens from the stands and as close as possible to the finish.

Night events must be photographed by available light. Nearly all tracks ban the use of flash or strobe because they could momentarily blind a driver. Choose a spot where the light level is its brightest. You may have to push fast pan film to the limit—about ASA 2000—to get acceptable pictures. For really bad light, try Kodak 2475 Recording film. It can be exposed at astronomical ratings of ASA 4000 or higher. The negatives will be extremely grainy, but you can make pictures that would be impossible with slower films.

MOTORCYCLE RACING

You can use the same photographic techniques to cover motorcycle racing, which consists of two distinct types of competition. There are high-speed contests, like those run by the American Motorcycle Association on its National Road Racing circuit at different tracks throughout North America. These races are comparable to the big, Indianapolis-type car races. Then there are the gruelling endurance races called "motocross." Motocross combines high speeds over a bone-breaking course filled with obstacles designed to separate a rider from his machine in the most violent manner. A professional motocross layout may include steep hills with ski-type jumps, water holes, mud holes, and fallen trees, individually or in combination. The picture possibilities are magnificent.

In addition to these rigidly programmed professional events, there are enough amateur and semipro motorcycle races held in this country

(Above) Motorcycles round a curve on flat track. Data: Nikon, 135mm lens, 1/250 sec. at f/3.5, Tri-X rated at ASA 1600, available light, developed in Acufine. (Over) Camera panned at a slow shutter speed to blur action. Data Nikon, 135mm lens, 1/15 sec. at f/11, Tri-X rated at ASA 1600, available light, developed in Acufine.

(Left) Motocross is a grueling endurance contest that combines high speeds with a rugged, twisting course laid out in difficult terrain. Here two cyclists negotiate a ski-type jump over the top of a hill. Data: motorized Nikon, 200mm lens, 1/1000 sec. at f/11, Tri-X. Photo by Steve Reyes, *Popular Cycling Magazine.*

to satisfy the most hardened action enthusiast. They include oval- and flat-track competition, hill climbs, and desert racing.

Competition is divided into different classifications, depending on the horsepower of the cycle as well as the experience of the rider. There are separate events for novice, intermediate, and advanced contestants, and sometimes a winner-take-all open category.

In photographing any motor sports events, a fresh and unusual approach is needed to avoid the clichéd, round-the-track pictures. Watch for that spectacular flip or collision, but also be aware of the artistic elements present — the colorful, blurred shapes careening into a turn, the patterns of light and shadow amid the dust, and the furious, head-on drive toward the finish line and victory circle with man the master of his machine.

CHAPTER 15

RODEO, HORSE SHOWS, AND THOROUGHBRED RACING

RODEO

Rodeo is a distinctly American form of insanity that originated somewhere in the Old West a little more than a century ago. No one is quite sure how it all got started. More than likely, the rodeo began during the legendary cattle drives of the 1860's and 1870's, when cowboys competed to see who could ride and rope the best. Today, a western rodeo may feature competition for all age levels, from grade school through college, with young contestants wrestling wild steers and hurtling from the backs of bucking horses and bulls like their pioneer ancestors.

At the professional level, 6,000 members of the Rodeo Cowboys Association, the governing body for the sport, compete in rodeo events throughout the United States and in the western provinces of Canada. It's a big business, and a top-ranked cowboy can earn over $50,000 per year. But it's a dangerous way to make a living. As in other violent sports, injuries and sometimes death are accepted risks. Broken arms, legs, and ribs are the rodeo's normal occupational hazards.

Besides the pros, there are numerous interscholastic and amateur rodeo organizations composed of cowboys and cowgirls from 6 to 60. In some western states, they stage a year-long round of competition including calf roping, bareback and saddle bronc riding, steer wrestling, and bull riding. These action-filled events can produce many spectacular photographs.

There are two schools of thought about covering a rodeo. One requires the photographer to be inside the arena during the riding events, working close to the chutes from which the animals and riders emerge. This method is favored by some courageous professionals who cover the

sport on a regular basis and develop great ability in dodging hoofs and horns. It is definitely not recommended for the average photographer. A wildly kicking horse or bull can inflict serious injuries on anyone in its path. The bulls are especially dangerous.

Usually of Brahma or mixed-Brahma stock, the evil-tempered bull packs close to a ton of horned fury above four deadly hoofs, and he has an acute aversion to photographers. The goal in this event, as in bronc riding, is for the contestant to stay on the bull for 8 seconds (6 seconds for girls and juniors under 14) and show as much style as possible while doing it. He can only hold on with one hand, or he is disqualified.

Besides his own skill, the rider depends on the rodeo clowns — his personal life preservers! If the cowboy is thrown, the bull will almost certainly attack him. It is here that the clowns enter, waving their arms in the bull's face and offering themselves as moving targets. Hopefully, they distract the beast while the cowboy (or photographer) scrambles to safety.

A bucking horse can be uncontrollable with a rider on his back, but once the rider is thrown, the horse, except for an occasional maverick, usually becomes quiet. The bull, however, remains thoroughly vicious and will do his best to stomp and gore a fallen rider.

The safest method of covering a rodeo is with a camera inside the arena and the cameraman outside, shooting through the perimeter fence. Try to locate a position across the arena facing the chute area. The action will be coming head-on as the broncs and bulls emerge. Many riders are thrown in the first few seconds, and opposite the chute area is an excellent location from which to record the spill. If the animals turn to the left or right, it is still possible to get many good shots. However, in the bareback and saddle bronc events, camera angles may be blocked by two or three mounted pick-up men who are there to pluck the contestant off his horse if he is fortunate enough to complete his eight-second ride. In this case, play the law of averages and wait for the next rider. There are usually plenty of chances to come up with an exciting picture.

If the opening in the fence is too small to push a lens through, seek a position at a slightly higher angle in the grandstand. You will be able to cover most of the action adequately with a medium-to-long telephoto lens (100–200mm).

A bareback bronc rider hits the dirt during a rodeo at National Horseman's Arena, Pueblo West, Colorado. Photo was made from across the arena facing the chutes from which the animals and riders emerge.
Data: Minolta, 200mm lens, 1/1000 sec. at f/11, Tri-X.

(Above) Cowboy Joe Dorenkamp demonstrates proper steer-wrestling, or bulldogging, technique in Colorado Championship Rodeo, Pueblo, Colorado. Long lenses are essential in covering this action, which usually takes place in the middle of the arena. Data: Minolta, 300mm lens, 1/1000 sec. at f/11, Tri-X.

(Left) Sheila Bussey, winner of the all-around cowgirl championship, ties legs of calf in All-Girls Rodeo at National Horseman's Arena, Pueblo West, Colorado. Data: Nikkormat, 200mm lens, 1/500 sec. at f/8, Tri-X, on a cloudy day.

Most rodeos feature a girls' barrel race in which contestants run their horses around three barrels placed in a triangular pattern inside the arena. Fastest time wins the event. Jerri Draper, 18, rounds the final barrel to win the event in the All-Girls Rodeo at National Horseman's Arena, Pueblo West, Colorado. Barrel racing produces fine pictures of individual horses and riders. Data: motorized Nikon, 200mm lens, 1/500 sec. at f/8, Tri-X.

Steer wrestling, or bulldogging, offers additional photographic opportunities. In this event, the cowboy has to jump from a galloping horse onto the neck of a running steer, and using the animal's horns for leverage, throw him to the ground. Since both horse and steer are racing at speeds up to 35 miles per hour, the slightest miscalculation by the rider can prove disastrous. Rodeo steers weigh upwards of 300 pounds and are equipped with needle-sharp horns. While these animals are not usually vicious, they can be extremely dangerous.

The steer is given a 10-foot lead out of the chute before the mounted cowboy is allowed to emerge. He depends on a fellow horseman, called a hazer, to ride close along the steer's right flank and keep him running in as straight a line as possible until the cowboy is in position to jump. The man who throws his steer in the shortest time wins the money. An experienced contestant can chase and bring down a steer in 10 seconds or less.

Shooting these fast-moving events calls for top shutter speeds to stop the action. The recommended speeds are $1/500$ sec. and $1/1000$ sec. For a change of pace, utilize the panning technique with slower shutter speeds, like $1/30$ sec. or $1/60$ sec., to graphically portray the action against a blurred background.

Calf and team roping round out the main events of a rodeo. In calf roping, the rider pursues a small calf that he is required to rope and throw in the shortest possible time, tying its legs together to complete the job. As in steer wrestling, the calf gets a head start to give him a chance to out-maneuver the horse, a frequent occurrence.

In team roping, two contestants go after a steer, one roping the head, the other his hind hooves. The team who accomplishes this task quickest wins the event. Roping, when done by experts, is a tremendous crowd pleaser.

Most rodeos feature a girls' barrel race. In this event, the riders race their horse around three barrels placed in a triangular pattern inside the arena. The contestant with the fastest time wins the race. This race provides plenty of chances for closeups of outstanding equestrian form.

Between events, concentrate on a variety of unposed photos of contestants' preparations—taping their hands, adjusting roping gear and saddles—and other fine details of the sport, all of which complement the action coverage.

The final word on rodeo photography belongs to a news syndicate cameraman who shall remain nameless. Never having covered a rodeo, he foolishly elected to shoot bull riding from the center of the arena. The first Brahma to be released from the chute promptly chose him for a target. The hapless photographer stood frozen with terror, unable to

J. D. Yates, 12-year-old champion steer roper, displays top form in winning the roping event of the Little Britches Rodeo at National Horseman's Arena, Pueblo West, Colorado. A telephoto lens pulled in the action from a camera position across the arena. Data: Minolta, 300mm lens, 1/1000 sec. at f/8, Tri-X.

lift his camera as the bull charged. Luckily, two rodeo clowns reached him before the bull did and distracted the Brahma long enough for our hero to regain his senses and escape over the fence. He headed for the exit, still trembling, and disappeared from view.

An hour later he was back in action, happily perched above the arena in lofty splendor and complete safety—in the bucket of a huge cherry-picker crane he had rented from a nearby construction yard!

HORSE SHOWS

Throughout history, wherever there have been horses, there have been men and women whose pride of ownership and competitive spirit have required them to exhibit their equestrian skills.

The horse-show photographer must keep a watchful eye on the movement of the contestants. The camera's shutter must be tripped at the exact instant when a horse's ears, feet, and tail are in the position that shows the animal at its best. To know what the correct position looks like, it is essential that the photographer know something about horses.

You can classify horse-show photographs in three distinct categories: the saddle horse, the jumper, and the hunter.

Saddle-Horse Competition

Saddle-horse competition is usually divided into two divisions, English and American Western, with the riders wearing the traditional clothing. Saddles are either English or Western, depending on the event. Horse and rider are judged on grace and style while performing at a walk, trot, or rapid canter. For riding pictures, a trotting or cantering horse is preferred because the animal appears at his best during these gaits. The legs are coordinated in a synchronized motion emphasizing the horse's most graceful rhythm.

A standing horse is best photographed at an angle that clearly shows both ears. An assistant can be used to attract the horse's attention. Just before you are ready to make the picture, have the assistant whistle softly or rattle pebbles in a tin can. The sudden noise will make the horse pick up his ears and hold his head erect, creating a more animated picture. A spectator or contestant who is not riding can act as assistant to the photographer. There are usually plenty of interested people around a horse show who are glad to lend a hand.

There are other small details that can improve or degrade the quality of a photograph; for example, a confusing background can destroy an otherwise good shot by distracting the viewer's eye from the graceful movements of a horse. Take care that trees and telephone

Jumping event in English-style horse show was photographed at about a 45-degree camera angle to the barrier. This location will show both horse and rider to good advantage. Data: Nikon, 105mm lens, 1/500 sec. at f/8, Kodak Ektacolor Professional Type S film. Black-and-white Panalure print from 35mm color negative.

poles don't stick out from a horse's head. Also, pay attention to the clothes the riders are wearing if you are shooting individual closeups in the formally structured English events. See that their clothing is arranged properly whenever possible — jackets buttoned, ties and hats on straight, and so forth. Since the riders are also judged on their personal appearance, they are naturally careful of their clothing.

Western Division events are designed to test the ability and manners of a horse trained in practical ranch work. Some of these events include tasks performed on the open range, like herding or roping cattle. These are not like rodeo events — there is no wild-bull or bronc riding here. The emphasis is on testing the skills of a trained horse going through his normal working routine.

Other Western events establish the rider's mastery of his mount in general horsemanship ranging from a walk to a gallop.

Jumper and Hunter Competition

Jumpers are the most photogenic of horses. They perform in the show ring where they are required to hurdle barriers from three to five feet high. In championship events, the barriers may go as high as seven feet to break a tie between two or more horses that have completed the course without a miss.

The obstacles vary from simple fence posts and rails to a nerve-wracking combination of stacked barrels and vertical walls, arranged in a twisting pattern with irregular distances between them so horse and rider must constantly readjust their pace.

The hunter-class horses are also jumpers, but their field of action is a measured course over a variety of obstacles in open country. Hunter competition simulates the traditional English fox hunt, in which teams of horsemen and dogs pursued the animal across miles of moors and farmland. The course is often condensed to fit within the boundaries of an arena. Horses are pitted against a variety of man-made and natural barriers including hedgerows and water holes.

In photographing a jumper, the best camera angle is about 45° to the barrier, or roughly a three-quarter front view. This angle will usually show all four legs of the horse as he completes the jump. A straight side view is sometimes interesting, but frequently does not show the configuration of the horse to good advantage. Head-on shots should be avoided. They tend to make the horse appear rather stubby and awkward. An exception to this principle would be a steeplechase event in which the horses are required to leap a fence and water hole. Sometimes a horse will trip and throw the rider. The resulting fall and splash will make a dynamic picture. In this case, a head-on view from a safe distance with a long lens is very effective.

In horse-show competition, $1/500$ sec. will stop just about any action encountered. There are many good subjects to be covered besides the jumpers: closeups of contestants grooming their horses before an event; judges scrutinizing the entries; ribbon and trophy winners receiving their awards. All these are interesting, behind-the-scenes angles that should not be ignored.

THOROUGHBRED RACING

Photography at the race track is far from easy. The major tracks are about one mile in circumference, and the best vantage points for shooting are off limits to nonaccredited cameramen.

Vic Stein, official photographer for Santa Anita and Hollywood Park race tracks in southern California, has covered over 50,000 thoroughbred races in a career spanning 3 decades. For the racing buff who enjoys following the horses with a camera, a personal account of his experiences is of particular interest:

First of all, if you are at a track that is as wide as ours, 85–90 feet, you must remain in the spectators' area behind the outside rail. This puts you at least 100 feet from the inside rail where the horses most generally run. For 35mm equipment, you will need at least a 135mm telephoto for a decent shot on a finish. If you want to bring in a favorite horse, a 200mm is ideal. Anything longer would be a bit too tight to show the entire horse. A longer lens, however, would be valuable for overhead shots from the grandstand if you are unable to get close to the outside rail.

To show the entire field of horses from a ground-level position at the rail, an 85–105mm lens gives you sort of a "wide-angle telephoto" view that can be remarkably effective. My personal choice is an 85–250mm zoom, which gives me all of the most-used focal lengths in one package.

Some of your best human-interest shots will be the fans around you. Most racing programs consist of seven or eight races including one big-money feature event. After you've shot a few finishes on the preliminary races, focus on the fans

Three thoroughbreds drive for the finish line in a close race. Remote-control camera was triggered by photographer 20 feet away to avoid possibility of scaring the horses and causing them to veer out of position. Data: motorized Nikon, 85-250mm zoom lens, 1/1000 sec. at f/9, Tri-X. Camera was placed on ground under the inside rail of track and prefocused on the spot where the horses would run. Photo by Vic Stein.

for some spectacular displays of emotion as they watch their hard-earned dollars riding to victory on a winner or going down the tubes in the back stretch.

We'll have three cameramen on an important race. The first man covers the finish at ground level from a point in front of the outside rail. This gives him a good side view of the horses crossing the finish line. He can also cover the turn into the final stretch if required. The second man is working from a five-foot platform across the track just behind the inside rail. He can get a different angle as the horses go past him after the start, the first time around, and also at the finish. The third man gets the start, if we need it, and also the final drive into the home stretch.

This arrangement gives us at least six or seven good action possibilities, and of course with motorized cameras, we have a large number of exposures from which to choose. There are also 10-foot camera platforms located at other points on the track — on the final stretch turn before the finish line and on the back stretch. This gives us additional angles with which to work.

One thing you have to do when you're on the platforms, since they're fairly close to the inside rail, is to remain perfectly still until all the horses pass. As a general rule, you're just shooting the lead horses. If you were to make a fast movement, the following horses might shy and throw their riders or veer out of position and lose a chance to win the race. Anything could happen. Thoroughbreds are skittish, high-strung animals and are easily spooked by an unexpected motion so close to them.

For the same reason, you cannot get within 20 feet of a racing horse at track level. Sometimes you want a low-angle, under-the-rail shot, which gives a dramatic, nearly straight-on look at the horses charging into the camera. To get this, a motorized camera is placed under the post of the inside rail, and triggered by a remote-control cord. You're never sure of what you've got until you see the negs, but you can get some beauties this way.

After the horses cross the finish line, they slow down gradually, taking another lap around as they trot back in front of the grandstand. The bright silks worn by the jockeys will make a good color shot. Then comes the traditional winner's circle photos with the owners and trainers grouped around the horse and jockey. Strobe fill-in is required because the winner's circle is always in deep shadow at both our tracks.

Our best pictures are serviced to local newspapers, the wire services, and horse-oriented publications. In addition, the owners, trainers, and jockeys all want prints of their favorite thoroughbreds for personal use. Our biggest problem is trying to do something different or original. There is still the same old oval, and the horses look the same year after year. We do have one thing going for us — every race is different to the extent that we never know what is going to happen. An unknown horse and jockey may suddenly emerge from the pack, running wide on the outside, and sweep the field. Positions change rapidly in the last 50 yards of the race, and the winning entry may not be out in front until they're almost to the finish line. We've got to be prepared for the unexpected.

CHAPTER 16

WATER SPORTS

The sea, with its variety of moods from windless calm to savage storms, has been a source of artistic inspiration to photographers since the era of Daguerre. Billowing white sails, etched against a blue sky, make a sight that moves even the most reluctant landlubber lensman to spirited action. Power boats, slicing the waves, make appealing shots for nautical enthusiasts. Regattas offer plenty of pictures of speeding boats fighting for the lead and tense moments at every turn. Water is photogenic too, and a quiet sea, lake, or stream that mirrors the neighboring landscape can be transformed into images of graceful beauty.

SAILING

Sidelighting or backlighting is the secret of interesting sailing pictures, bringing out the texture of glistening water and providing a brilliant setting for the boat. A light-yellow or orange filter will naturally darken the sky on a bright day. A red filter will intensify the dramatic effect and is useful in scenic shots where a boat is silhouetted against the light. Because of the large amount of reflected light on water, you may lose only a one-half stop in securing normal exposure. Bracket whenever you can for insurance.

To photograph sailing races, use a power boat whenever possible. It is extremely maneuverable and will provide great flexibility in camera angles while following the racing fleet around the course. Even if you are an experienced yachtsman, it is wise to take another person along to run the boat while you concentrate on the camera. At most harbors or

Aerial view of sailboats on Lake Havasu, Arizona, was made from a helicopter. Wind-whipped waves create an interesting pattern of light and shadow. Data: Pentax, 105mm lens, 1/1000 sec. at f/16, Tri-X. Helicopter was maneuvered by pilot to obtain a camera angle in which the boats were backlit.

(Above) A sailor clings to a line from his capsized Hobie Cat during a regatta on Lake Havasu, Arizona. Data: Nikon, 105mm lens, 1/500 sec. at f/16, Tri-X.

(Left) Hobie Cat sailboat heels into the wind during a regatta on Lake Havasu, Arizona. Data: Nikon, 200mm lens, 1/1000 sec. at f/11, Tri-X. Photo made from speedboat following the racing fleet.

A fleet of Hobie Cat sailboats lie dead in the water during a regatta on Lake Havasu, Arizona. Desert winds suddenly faded, causing this nautical traffic jam on the quiet waters of the lake. Data: Nikon, 50mm lens, 1/500 sec. at f/11, Tri-X, light-yellow (K-2) filter.

marinas, there are small power boats available for rental with an experienced driver who handles the boat. Boat owners are invariably a friendly bunch, and they will frequently invite you aboard as their guest to photograph the race. Under these conditions, it is customary to offer payment for fuel or at least to shoot a few pictures of your host in appreciation of his hospitality.

Sailing races, or regattas, are held over a measured course, which may be several miles in length. Take a position near one of the buoys marking a turn, and catch the boats scrambling for position. If there is a strong wind blowing, things can get pretty hectic, with sailors hiked out (suspended over the sides) and leaning dangerously close to the turbulent waves as they trim the sails to coax the last ounce of performance from their craft. In the small catamaran classes, it is not unusual for a boat to capsize, dunking the crew in the water. In most cases, only feelings are hurt, but occasionally someone is injured. This unhappy moment is newsworthy and should be recorded to round out race coverage. In formal competition, patrol boats are stationed in key positions around the course and always move in swiftly to assist any boat in distress. Medium-to-long telephoto lenses (100–300mm) are essential to cover the action from a safe distance because they prevent any interference with the conduct of the race.

Ocean sailing races may be held several miles offshore, making them impossible to photograph without using a boat. On the other hand, sailing races at inland lakes or rivers frequently offer a variety of good onshore camera positions. There may be a beach or hillside that overlooks the race course where a long lens may be effectively utilized. You can tie in these shots with close-up surface photos taken from a boat for a complete story.

Wind-whipped spray and sand are deadly enemies to intricate camera mechanisms. Salt-water spray is terribly corrosive to metal and leather. Keep your equipment protected in a plastic bag until you're ready to shoot, and carry a small, soft cotton towel to wipe off excess spray. Lenses should be covered by a UV or Skylight filter to keep them dry. These clear filters are always required for color to reduce the heavy blue prevalent in marine scenes.

For increased protection on rainy days, tape a plastic bag over the camera, leaving small holes for the lens, viewfinder, shutter release, and film advance. Carry a second plastic bag large enough to hold the camera, and use it to change film. These arrangements are somewhat clumsy and will slow you down, but they can prevent an expensive camera-repair bill if your gear gets soaked.

POWERBOAT RACING

Powerboat racing is photographed utilizing the same techniques as for sailing events. However, this sport can be extremely dangerous to cover because of the tremendous speeds involved. You must stay well clear of the racecourse, which may vary in length depending on the class of boats entered. Long focal-length lenses are essential. Boat drivers are constantly busy coping with the demands of a sensitive, high-powered racing hull, traveling at speeds in excess of 100 miles per hour. A driver's visibility is often hampered by flying spray, and it may be impossible to see a small boat that blunders onto the course. The results of such a collision could be fatal. For this reason, surface coverage of a powerboat race is usually restricted by race officials to a very small number of press boats, manned by highly experienced skippers.

Most powerboat races are held with some consideration for the spectators, at least for the start and finish. There may be a position along the shore that affords a good camera angle. It is necessary to arrive early and inspect the area in order to find the best possible location.

WATER SKIING

Water-ski speed competition is best photographed from a boat running alongside the skiers, from 50–100 feet away. This method is fine if the water is calm. However, if it gets choppy, the camera boat will be lurching all over the waves, and good photography is extremely difficult. Fast shutter speeds, seldom any slower than $^1/_{500}$ sec., are required to avoid image-spoiling camera movement. In this situation, take a position near a turn and let the action come to you. Skiers are most likely to wipe out at this point, and the resulting fall and splash can be sensational.

Trick water-ski events are easy to photograph from the stern of the boat pulling the contestant. Permission must be obtained in advance from the individual boat drivers. They are frequently publicity conscious and will be most cooperative. Trick skiing offers a fascinating array of pictures. There are gymnastics and dance routines, singles and doubles jumping events, slalom (one-foot), and even barefoot skiing. The competition is held with the boat running at slow speeds (18–20 miles per hour) with contestants receiving points for accuracy and style similar to a ballet dancer or ice skater. In trick events, the skiers work with shorter tow lines for ease in handling (40–75 feet) as compared with the 150- or 200-foot lines necessary to endure the stress of speed competition. A 135mm or 200mm lens will pull in a good-sized image of the skier when you are working from his tow boat.

SURFING

A popular water sport in coastal areas, surfing is tough to photograph without a super-long lens because the action takes place so far out in the water. Occasionally, a nearby pier or jetty will give you a closer view so you can use a 200mm lens; but most surfing locations

Aerial shot of unique "pickle fork" outboard racer was made from a helicopter while covering the Outboard World Championship on Lake Havasu, Arizona. Data: motorized Nikon, 200mm lens, 1/1000 sec. at f/8, Tri-X, low-level aerial shot on cloudy day. Reproduced courtesy of Laurence Laurie & Associates.

John Arendsen, Los Angeles, California, tried to water ski from a stepladder mounted on a sheet of heavy-duty plywood at Canyon Lake, California, in the trick water-skiing tournament. The novel experiment failed, and John got a dunking. Data: motorized Nikon, 105mm lens, 1/1000 sec. at f/11, Tri-X. Photos were made from stern of speedboat towing the skier.

require telephotos ranging from 400mm to a collossal 1000mm! A sturdy tripod is your number one accessory. Keep a low angle. The closer the lens is to the water, the higher and more exciting the waves will appear.

One way to beat the giant-lens requirement is to put your camera in an underwater housing or to use a special waterproof camera like the Nikonos. This costly gear can often be rented from marine dealers who supply equipment for surfers and skin divers. You can work in shallow water and catch the surfers as they approach.

(Pp 132-135) In this sequence, Walt Cook, Redondo Beach, California, shows how to water ski on his bare feet at 40 miles per hour during trick water-skiing tournament on Canyon Lake, California. First, Cooke kicks off his water ski and skis on his bare feet. He loses his balance and starts to fall. Finally, he winds up in the lake with a cloud of spray. Data: motorized Nikon, 200mm lens, 1/1000 sec. at f/11, Tri-X. Photos were made from another speedboat running alongside the water skier about 80 feet away. This type of picture requires the cooperation of a skilled boat driver working with the photographer.

Some adventurous photographers have been known to paddle out on surfboards themselves to be in the center of the action. This practice is not advisable for the novice. A breaking wave may knock you off the board, which then becomes an unguided missile hurtling across the water. Even experienced surfers have been clobbered by their own boards in a spill.

Working close to the surfers with wide-angle lenses to medium telephotos offers some advantages in gaining a dramatic perspective, but it is risky. Most photographers on assignment for surfing magazines favor the long-lens method from the shore to meet the demands of their highly specialized publications.

SWIMMING AND DIVING

Swimming, as a competitive sport, has had a rapid development in recent years, with many high schools and colleges assembling teams. The standard set of swimming distances for racing ranges from 50–880 yards. Events include the four standard methods of swimming—backstroke, breast stroke, free style, and butterfly. The sport is tricky to photograph because the swimmers' faces are obscured by water or flailing arms for much of the time. You have to watch your angles carefully and shoot when their faces are visible. To zero-in on individual contestants, telephoto lenses are mandatory. It takes a lot of film and good luck to cover a swim meet, and the percentage of successful pictures is lower than normal.

If you are concentrating on one particular swimmer, play it safe and shoot as he dives into the pool at the beginning of a race, thereby giving you at least one shot where his face is sure to be seen. Then try to show him competing against the other swimmers.

When a swimmer completes a lap, he must smoothly reverse direction by touching the end of the pool and propelling himself backward to begin the next lap. His face may be visible for several seconds as he turns around, giving you another chance for a picture.

Diving is a beautiful sport to watch and to photograph. The graceful bodies of athletes plunging into the blue, translucent water are sometimes exquisitely perfect in form.

A surfer carries his board into the Pacific Ocean at Malibu, California. Use of backlighting and inclusion of the sun in the picture created an effective silhouette. Data: Nikon, 35mm lens, 1/1000 sec. at f/16, Tri-X. Photo by Bill Beebe.

(Above) Roland Matthes, East Germany, wins the 100 meters men's backstroke and sets a new Olympic record at the 1972 Munich Games. Data: 35mm camera, telephoto lens, fast pan film. UPI photo.

(Right) Defending Olympic platform diving champion Klaus Dibiasi, Italy, performs a 1½ fold inward somersault during the men's platform diving competition at Munich. Data: 35mm camera, telephoto lens, fast pan film. UPI photo.

Competitive diving events are held in three stages: from a low board, about 4 feet above the water; from a high board, set at 9 or 10 feet; and from a high platform, positioned from 15–32 feet above the water. Divers compete in their specialties and are judged for correctness of form in the execution of their dives. Three basic styles of diving are the forward swan and somersault, the back somersault, and the gainer (twist) dives. Variations on the twist theme include the half- and full gainer and the back jackknife. Any of these dives will present an interesting photo.

On the high board and platform, multiple aerobatic routines are often combined in a single, twisting dive, presenting exceptional photographic opportunities. A motorized camera is desirable, but not absolutely necessary. Most contestants are required to make two or three dives for the judges, which gives you more chances to shoot. With rapid-wind levers on most cameras, it is possible to get more than one picture on each dive, even without a motor.

CHAPTER 17

SKI PHOTOGRAPHY

Shooting ski pictures is fun. It may take strenuous physical effort at times, but the photographer who is willing to extend himself will be amply rewarded. There are few subjects more splendidly exhilarating than a skier flashing across a brilliant, sun-drenched mountain slope on a carpet of glistening snow or soaring into space from a steep precipice. These are but a few of the opportunities awaiting anyone who will venture out into the chill mountain air.

A number of top-notch sports photographers handle skiing assignments on a regular basis. Two of these veterans are Jack Sheedy and George Long, West Coast photographers for *Sports Illustrated*. Since they are both avid skiers as well, their techniques and advice will be of interest. In an interview on ski photography, Sheedy and Long had this to say:

To enjoy the excitement of ski photography, it is not necessary to be a skier yourself, but it is helpful, especially in getting to remote locations in rugged terrain where hiking is impossible without special snow shoes. Also, walking through snow in ordinary shoes and boots leaves deep holes that can cause a speeding skier to fall. At some ski runs, the official ski patrol bars entry to persons without the proper footware.

There are many ways for non-skiers to make good action shots. If you are at a ski resort or other designated skiing area, most of the beginner and intermediate runs will be within walking distance or easily accessible by a chair lift, which is used to transport skiers up the slopes. It is a simple matter to ride the lift up and down to position yourself to good advantage.

Early in the morning or late in the afternoon is the best time to shoot. The sun is at a low angle, producing longer shadows and sharper textures on the snow. Avoid the middle of the day when the sun is high in the sky. The noon lighting tends to be rather dull and lifeless. This is the time to shoot the skiers relaxing around the lodge — perhaps a picnic lunch in the snow or pretty girls frolicking in their colorful stretch pants. These little, added details brighten your action coverage.

If you are lucky enough to be out just after a fresh snowfall, the new powdery snow is an added bonus. Find a point where a skier is making a turn or coming across a ridge against the skyline. A downhill slalom course is another good location. Cover it from the outside of the turns to catch the flying snow. A skier jumping a mogul, a bump of snow, will also be interesting.

Medium-long telephoto lenses (100–200mm) will let you photograph a skier from a safe distance and still produce a good-size negative image. It's not a good idea to get too close to a downhill run, especially when covering competitive events. Fast-moving skiers occasionally get out of control and may land in your lap if you are not careful. Zoom lenses are ideal, if you have one, because they let you cover more of the action from one location. For general shooting, a normal or wide-angle lens is useful for showing the skiers against scenic mountain backgrounds. A particularly good location would be at a jump on the crest of a hill. Work from behind the jump as the skier takes off and catch him in mid-air with the valley below him. It may even be possible to include the ski resort or town in the background, adding interest to the picture.

Panning the camera with the skier is a good way to create a sense of speed. Try different shutter speeds starting at $1/30$ sec. or $1/60$ sec. to get some blur in the picture. If you prefer to stop the action, $1/250$ sec. or $1/500$ sec. will freeze the skier against a suitably blurred background, suggesting a feeling of motion. It isn't necessary to shoot everything at $1/1000$ sec. once you learn how to pan properly. Working at the slower shutter speeds frequently produces a much more meaningful picture.

If you are working with a competent skier who can handle himself on the slopes, it is possible to set up a good shot by

having him make a jump or sharp turn at a predetermined point, kicking up a spray of snow. You'll have many opportunities to do this during a skiing session.

Another possibility is shooting across a gully at a skier coming down the other side. This usually requires a fairly long lens, over 200mm, but it can produce an interesting perspective because the camera angle will be above the skier.

Bright sun on snow can lead to serious exposure problems due to the intensity of the light. You can figure on at least one or two stops more light in most situations. For black-and-white, we like to use Tri-X because it has a longer tonal scale and is much less contrasty than slower films, like Plus-X or Panatomic-X. Development is in D-76, 1:1, or Microdol-X, 1:3, as recommended by the manufacturer. The diluted developer gives us better gradation than straight "soup" (slang for developer) would. Proper exposure is based on shadow areas, and we sometimes reduce development times 10–25 percent to cut contrast. This technique requires some experimentation for best results. It helps to shoot a test roll, if possible, and to process it before you run the important stuff.

A light-yellow filter will darken the sky and give better separation between the snow and sky. An orange or red filter produces even darker skies and increases the dramatic effect. They are especially useful in overall scenic views and also in close-up shots of skiers when you want to include the sun in the picture. This is easy to do with a wide-angle lens. Try to backlight the action, silhouetting the skiers against the sky. Stopping the lens down to a fairly small aperture, like f/16 or f/22, may produce a beautiful star-burst effect on the film. This is caused by the rays of the sun reflecting through the diaphragm blades. Some photographers prefer to use a special star filter, or a fine piece of wire mesh in front of the lens, for consistent results. This technique is also very effective with color films, without using the black-and-white filters.

For color, Kodachrome 25 is preferred because of its fine grain and sharpness. Kodachrome 64 or Ektachrome-X is used when more speed is required at low light levels. In the

Light falling snow does not affect the enthusiasm of skier sailing off jump during freestyle contest at Heavenly Valley, California. Note the two photographers lying on their backs in the snow to shoot jump from a low angle. Data: 35mm camera, telephoto lens, Tri-X. Photo by South Lake Tahoe News Service.

A skier bends into a turn in downhill slalom course during Olympic trials at Squaw Valley, California. Data: motorized Nikon, 300mm lens, 1/500 sec. at f/8. Black-and-white print from Ektachrome-X transparency. Photo by Sheedy and Long.

mountains, you have a huge amount of ultraviolet light at high altitudes, and a Skylight filter is essential to hold down the excessive blue cast. This is very important in warming up shadow areas.

For distant backlighted subjects, reasonably accurate exposure readings can be made from the shadow side of your hand. Remember this trick when you are faced with a subject you can't get close to. Bracket exposures in one-half stop increments whenever possible. This will insure good results in tricky lighting situations.

Wrap your equipment in a lint-free towel to protect it when you are not shooting. If you do ski, a small belt or backpack will protect your camera and lenses from moisture. Wrapping your gear in small pieces of foam rubber helps cushion the bumps. Some photographers ski with a camera on a neck strap tucked inside their parka where it is protected and warm. This is fine if you are a fairly good skier and don't fall too often, but it is not recommended for beginners.

Whatever you do, never, never take your camera indoors if you intend to shoot outside within a short time. Condensation will form on all metal parts as well as the lens, even penetrating to the inner elements where it can't be seen. This can put you out of action for quite a while.

Friendly tips: If you are using a motorized camera, remember that cold weather will cause the batteries to slow down, and you may not get the same frame-per-second rate you are used to getting. It is a good idea to keep a spare set of batteries inside your parka where they will stay warm. Alternate them with the batteries in the motor as necessary. Shutters also lose some of their efficiency in extreme cold, which may cause exposure problems. Again, bracket exposures as much as possible.

Don't neglect your physical comfort. Allow ample time to move around if you are changing locations. Rapid exertion in icy, thin air at high altitudes may cause severe shortness of breath, headaches, and dizziness. Give your body a chance to become acclimatized.

Lightweight silk or cotton gloves will protect your hands and still permit efficient handling of camera controls. Avoid having the camera come in contact with bare skin. In below-freezing temperatures, metal welds itself to flesh, and you risk losing a big chunk of whatever is stuck to the camera. Unwary lensmen have lost portions of their fingers, noses, lips, and even tongues!

For prolonged shooting sessions, a pocket hand warmer is a valuable companion. They are available at ski equipment dealers and most sporting goods stores.

Use caution in advancing or rewinding film in cold, dry weather to prevent the buildup of static electricity, which can result in streaks and blotches on the emulsion. Film also becomes brittle under these conditions and may break if it is moved too quickly.

When covering ski racing, some of your best pictures will be at the finish line showing the varied emotions of contestants and fans. The tension of competition and the drama of victory or defeat are worthy subjects.

Look for other winter sports like ice skating or tobogganing that may be going on in the same area as skiing. They have a great potential for impressive pictures. You may apply the same principles as in covering skiing.

Knowing your subject and your equipment will pay dividends. It may seem difficult at first, but keep trying. You will learn from your early mistakes and gradually acquire the know-how to achieve good results. Whether you're shooting for fun or as part of your job, there are a lot of good ski pictures waiting out there in the mountains.

CHAPTER 18

HUNTING AND FISHING

PHOTOGRAPHING THE HUNT

Anxiously, you squat down in your blind. There in the misty distance, a dozen wavering gray specks are racing toward you. Silently, you wait, distinctly hearing the beat of wings as the specks grow larger. Canada Geese glide down to inspect the wooden decoys nesting on glassy water just 30 feet away. Now they're in range. Sighting on the leader, you rise up and let him have it.

But there's no blast of a shotgun. No birds falling. Only the quiet click of a camera shutter breaks the silence. You won't know until your film is developed whether you have missed or scored a direct hit. That's one of the unique attractions about hunting wildlife with a camera.

It is an outdoor activity that can be pursued at any time, without respect to season. And there is no limit to the game you can bag. In contrast, the gun-bearing hunter must abide by strict conservation laws that severely limit the amount and type of game he may take.

A complete knowledge of wildlife is not essential, but it does help if you have some understanding of the habits of your photographic quarry, whether it be bird or mammal. A trip to the local library or a friend who is an experienced hunter can often supply the information you need.

Perhaps you have observed nesting waterfowl or the great masses of ducks and geese that wing south every autumn and return north each spring. These fast-flying birds make fascinating pattern silhouettes against the sky.

If you live close to one of the great migratory flyways, you're in luck. If not, perhaps there is a lake or river nearby containing various species of waterfowl just waiting to be photographed.

(Above) Migrating snow geese make an appealing picture for the sportsman/photographer. Telephoto lenses are usually necessary for best results, since it is difficult to get close to these birds without scaring them away. Data: Nikon, 200mm lens, 1/1000 sec. at f/11, Tri-X. Photo by Bill Beebe.

(Left) A golden-mantled marmot emerges from its hiding place to surprise the cameraman who made a "grab" shot from 12 feet away before the animal could run. Photo was taken during a hunting trip in British Columbia, Canada. Data: Nikon, 200mm lens, 1/1000 sec. at f/5.6, Tri-X, overcast day. Photo by Bill Beebe.

Maybe you're the rugged type who enjoys backpacking into the high country to take game with both gun and camera. A photographic record of your hunting trip will provide many hours of enjoyment in the long winter evenings when the experience is just a dim remembrance.

To the sportsman who takes his photography seriously, a fine series of pictures is as good as a bag of quail or a record deer. Don't be content with a dull shot of a hunter posing with the game he killed. Give yourself an assignment to tell a story with pictures.

Start at home and plan the initial shot of the hunters preparing for a trip, say a typical deer shoot. Picture the men packing their car and starting out in the early morning. Include shots of the country in which the deer is hunted, perhaps with a hunter in the foreground, rifle slung over his shoulder, searching the distant terrain with powerful binoculars.

It takes a lot of luck (and long lenses) to film an actual kill, which may occur several hundred yards from the camera. It isn't easy to move agilely over rough ground, burdened with camera and hunting equipment; but capturing such a scene will result in a rare photographic prize. This kind of shot is seldom captured even by professional wildlife cameramen.

The final pictures in the series will show the hunters wrestling their kill back to civilization, a sometimes back-breaking chore made even more difficult by rugged terrain. Unless you need fill-in shots to complete a sequence, avoid posed pictures. Sometimes it is necessary to reenact a bit of action you missed, but this should be avoided if at all possible. Strive for naturally informal shots, they have far wider appeal than most posed scenes.

If the hunt is not successful and you have neither pictures nor deer, take consolation in the fact that you have received a lot of healthy outdoor exercise.

FRESH WATER FISHING

Fish are early risers. In most areas, the dawn hours produce the best fishing, and the photographer who is angling for pictures must arise at the most inconvenient times. However, if your favorite fishing spot is a mountain stream or lake at high altitudes (5,000 feet or more),

Sportsman/photographer Bill Beebe, at right, set his camera on a nearby rock and used the self-timer to make this shot of hunting guide Wilfred Lee and himself hauling dead mountain goats back to camp during hunting trip in British Columbia, Canada. Data: Rolleiflex, 80mm lens, 1/125 sec. at f/16 with self-timer, Tri-X, overcast day. Photo by Bill Beebe.

the finny creatures may not feel like biting until around noon, when the sun has heated the water to a comfortable temperature.

Late afternoon and early evening are also a time of active feeding, when the big ones come out of the deep water to cruise the shallows in search of a meal. Fish are afraid of bright sunlight because it makes them more visible to their natural enemies—birds, animals, and man. They prefer to lurk in dark places beneath the surface to keep out of danger. That's why the two choice times for fishing are early morning and evening, when the sun has left the surface and the light is low.

Do not think that it is impossible to catch fish (and pictures) at other times of day—far from it. Fish behavior, like human behavior, is often unpredictable; you can never tell where or when a hungry one will rise to take the bait.

If you enjoy fishing as well as photography, it's not easy to share angling time with your camera. Try to spend a few moments recording the scenic features of your fishing area or shooting a companion trying to land a squirming bass or trout. Such pictures will be remembered long after the trip is ended.

Don't be satisfied with typical record shots like a grinning angler holding up a string of dead fish. Such pictures are equally dead. You can do better. Highlight your fishing trip in stages as they occur. This is not as hard as it first might appear.

The opening shot might show the preparations underway, with rods and reels being readied. The next is a closeup of your wife or fishing companions loading the car or hitching a boat trailer. At the fishing grounds, capture the anglers assembling their gear or casting lures into the water. A long shot nicely framed through a tree limb or some shoreline foliage will add foreground interest to this sequence of pictures.

Although some sportsmen/photographers are versatile enough to operate a camera with one hand while battling a hooked fish with the other, most fishing action pictures require two people, one angler handling the rod and the other concentrating on the camera.

To record fishing action from a boat, a wide-angle lens is desirable because of its great depth-of-field characteristics. It is possible to photograph your fishing partner only a few feet away and get him sharp along with the surrounding water or scenic background. A 28mm lens on 35mm equipment is ideal for close work. For the 2¼" format, a 50mm or 55mm lens will give comparable results.

Fisherman with huge trout was photographed on a fishing trip in British Columbia, Canada. A low camera angle was used to emphasize the bulk of the fish. Data: Rolleiflex, 80mm lens, 1/250 sec. at f/16, Tri-X. Photo by Bill Beebe.

The cameraman should sit in the opposite end of the boat, as far away from the angler as possible. If a skiff or outboard motorboat is used, the angler might sit in the stern, facing forward, while the photographer remains in the bow. This allows shooting to either side of the boat.

Keep the camera ready at all times — perhaps tucked loosely in its case, stowed in a plastic bag under the boat seat, or strapped around your neck where it can be swiveled into action at the first hint of a fin. Don't forget to place a UV or Skylight filter over the lens to protect it from flying spray.

When shooting from a moving boat, shutter speeds of $1/500$ sec. or even $1/1000$ sec. are advisable to offset the vibration or sudden lurching of the craft at the time the shutter is released. Never rest the camera on any part of the boat. Keep it tucked firmly against your cheek, with elbows pressed against your body to keep as steady as possible.

Show your fishing partner casting. Focus on his hands where they grip the rod or on the point where the line enters the water if it is close to the boat, then settle back and wait. If your luck is good, it won't be too long before a strike is felt. The angler gives a slight upward thrust with the rod to set the hook, and the fun begins.

Take a shot of his excited face as he struggles to land the fish, pumping the rod up and down while reeling in swiftly. Be prepared for a quick shot as the fish surfaces. Some fresh water gamefish, like black bass and trout, may leap two or three times before finally giving up. A sharp photo of a leaping fish is indeed a rare prize.

Not until the film is developed does the photographer know the strange images he may have caught and the great ones that got away. More than likely, you'll have to be content with a less-than-spectacular shot of a fisherman pulling his catch into the boat or hoisting it aboard with a small hand net. But keep trying. In fishing, as in other sports, avoid shooting the commonplace from the same old angle. Looking for new photographic approaches means more hard work, but when you finally succeed in coming up with something different, the results more than justify the extra effort.

SALT WATER FISHING

If you are fortunate enough to live along either coast or within comfortable traveling distance, an ocean fishing journey will prove a real photographic challenge. Salt water gamefish are usually larger and meaner than their fresh water cousins, putting up a savage struggle when hooked. Larger species such as tarpon, sailfish, and marlin are noted for frenzied aerial acrobatics that require split-second timing to

(Right) Backlighting and a yellow filter transformed an ordinary shot of a surf fisherman into a scene of beauty. The sun was included in the picture area to increase the dramatic effect. Data: Rolleiflex, 80mm lens, 1/500 sec. at f/22, with light-yellow (K-2) filter, Tri-X. Photo by Bill Beebe.

(Below) A large black marlin leaps from the water as it is gaffed by fisherman preparing to haul it into the boat. Photo was taken on a fishing trip on the Pacific Ocean off the coast of Mexico. Hooked marlin frequently jump like this and make exciting subjects if you can catch them in time. Data: Leica, 50mm lens, 1/500 sec. at f/8, Plus-X. Photo by Al Tetzlaf, courtesy of Aeronaves de Mexico.

photograph. Others, like sharks and barracuda, are downright dangerous and should be treated with great caution. Many an angler has known moments of terror with just a small shark or 'cuda thrashing around in the bottom of his boat and trying to bite everything in sight. The big ones are deadly even when dispatched with a high-powered rifle slug through the head. The violent convulsions of a dying shark can devastate a small boat and its occupants. Reflex muscular actions may also cause them to bite long after death has occurred.

Other salt water specimens, like albacore, bonito, bonefish, tuna, yellowtail, and wahoo, are commonly taken by sportfishing boats and make good camera subjects as well. On an ocean-going vessel, the action is more difficult to handle because the water is usually rougher, even just a few miles offshore. Steady camera technique becomes a real problem. Plant yourself firmly on the deck, with knees and hips cushioning the bumps. In very choppy water, it may be impossible to stand for any length of time. Try bracing yourself against a stanchion or ladder to secure a good foothold.

Besides making it difficult to photograph, rough seas may cause a classic case of *mal de mer*, or acute seasickness. Carry some Dramamine or other type of anti-nausea pill to ward off the effects of a queasy stomach. Your doctor can prescribe adequate medication before you depart on a deep-water photo session.

Telephoto lenses are essential in photographing the larger gamefish. Anglers must work with much longer lines than in other types of fishing, and the best action may take place at distances over 200 feet when the hooked fish breaks water. A leaping marlin or sailfish may be airborne for several seconds or for just a brief instant. You never know.

As the tiring fish is reeled closer to the boat, change your focus accordingly to keep him sharp. Watch the line where it enters the water. The fish may rocket skyward, without warning, in a frantic effort to break free. By this time, however, most of his strength is usually gone, and he lies motionless just below the surface. Show the muscle-wrenching efforts of the crew gaffing and hauling the big fish safely aboard. A final shot of the happy fisherman examining his prize completes the story.

Sparkling highlights on water near fisherman were captured with a wide-angle lens stopped down to its smallest aperture. This created a starburst effect from each pinpoint light source, as strong sunlight reflected through blades of the diaphragm. This effect is possible in back-lit pictures when the sun is low on the horizon—just after sunrise or before sunset as in this shot. Exposure was timed to include boat passing in background. Data: Nikon, 28mm lens, 1/1000 sec. at f/16, Tri-X. A UV filter protected the lens from spray but did not affect exposure.

CHAPTER 19

SHOOT SPORTS FROM YOUR SEAT

The dream of every budding sports photographer is to obtain press credentials for a major athletic event. This is a giant step, in his mind, into the privileged world of the professional news or magazine cameraman. But not everyone can be allowed on the sidelines or into the press box at a big-time sports contest. Credentials must be rigidly controlled by the officials. If not, there would be so many people crowding the playing field that there would be no room for the athletes.

But what if you are just getting started in photography and don't have any affiliation that would entitle you to a press pass? The answer is simple: Buy a ticket. With a telephoto lens, you can cover almost any sports event from your seat, provided you are reasonably close to the action. How close? That depends on the sport and the focal length of your longest lens.

The first rule is to buy the best seat you can afford, as close to the playing field as possible. Try to pick a seat on an aisle or in the first row of a balcony. If you have an unobstructed view, you minimize the possibility of excited fans jumping in front of the lens when an exciting play takes place. This is the ideal location but one that is not easy to obtain at a popular sports attraction where tickets are at a premium.

Sports like football, baseball, auto and motorcycle racing, where the action is fairly distant from most of the spectators, require at least a 200mm lens on a 35mm camera. Even then, you may be limited to more or less general views of the event. A 300mm lens gives you a better chance for an exciting closeup. At some of the small stadiums the crowd is closer to the field, and a 135mm lens may be sufficient.

Basketball, hockey, and track may be adequately filmed with 85–135mm lenses if your seat is within 100 feet of the area you wish to cover. Zoom lenses are ideal except that most of them are limited to a maximum aperture of around $f/3.5$. This may be too slow for shooting color in available light.

A 300mm or 400mm lens is needed if you're located in the middle or upper rows of a large stadium. And don't forget the opportunities afforded by the crowd around you. A second camera with a normal or wide-angle lens is useful for quick shots of the fans' reactions.

Telephotos longer than 400mm are extremely difficult to use when working from a crowd. The guy in the seat ahead may strongly object to having a big cannon of a lens poking over his shoulder all day. The short-barrel mirror telephotos of 500mm or more are an exception, but their complex optical systems make them difficult to focus at low light levels and very shaky to hand hold.

With any long lens, a shoulder brace or monopod is helpful in obtaining maximum steadiness. Most sports arenas or stadiums forbid the use of tripods in the aisles between rows of seats where someone might trip over them.

If you don't own a super-long lens, a $2\times$ tele-extender, which doubles the focal length of your normal lens or medium telephoto, is a fine investment. The extender reduces the speed of your prime lens by one or more stops. It also degrades image sharpness at the corners of the negative, but this valuable accessory will greatly increase the distance at which you may work.

Working from an elevated position within the grandstand has its advantages for certain sports, like basketball and hockey. You can pick up a good deal of reflected light from the ice or the highly polished basketball court — up to a full stop, depending on the illumination of the particular arena. A word of caution here: Through-the-lens or reflected-light meters may give inflated readings in this type of situation, leading to severe underexposure if followed. Adjust the exposure for the skin tones of the athletes, and bracket whenever you can. Incident-light, or spot, meters, with their narrow acceptance angles, are generally more accurate if used correctly.

Don't envy the news photographers you see at work on the sidelines or in the press box. You have one big advantage over them: You can concentrate freely on subjects that interest you, without regard to deadlines or the need to satisfy a cranky editor. Shooting sports events from your seat requires practice and a modest helping of good luck. Even from a high-level seat in the center of a crowd, you might produce a smash picture with an angle nobody else can duplicate. You will probably lose a few exposures to the jumpers, or excited fans, getting in front of your lens. By observing the action and waiting for the right moment, however, you'll be rewarded with some thrilling pictures that you'll be proud to exhibit anywhere.

INDEX